A PRACTICAL GUIDE TO NEGOTIATION

A PRACTICAL GUIDE TO NEGOTIATION

THOMAS F. GUERNSEY
Dean and Professor of Law
Southern Illinois University

National Institute for Trial Advocacy

Reproduction Permission
National Institute for Trial Advocacy
1602 North Ironwood
South Bend, Indiana 46530
(800) 225-6482
Fax (219) 282-1263
E-mail nita.1@nd.edu

Guernsey, Thomas F., *A Practical Guide to Negotiation* (NITA, 1996).

ISBN 1-55681-500-X

To Ruth and Lori Guernsey and Sue Gordon

Contents

Chapter 8: Crisis and Outcome

Chapter 9: Ethical Considerations

PREFACE

Whether you are handling the purchase of property for a major real estate development, trying to reach agreement in a bank merger, putting together a joint venture, negotiating with opposing counsel in a medical malpractice case, dealing with a disgruntled office employee, or negotiating your own partnership agreement with a colleague, lawyers spend much of their time negotiating.

Viewed broadly, negotiation is the process by which two or more parties solve a particular problem over which they may have competing interests, needs, or desires. Negotiation obviously takes place within a wide variety of relationships and under a wide variety of circumstances. Throughout all negotiations, however, there remains a common thread. In each circumstance, people come together with potentially different goals and attempt to solve a specific problem. The tone may be quite different when negotiating on behalf of a client in a lawsuit than when negotiating for purchasing a car. The process, as we shall see, however, is essentially the same.

This book proceeds on the premise that negotiation ought to be a process in which you make conscious, thoughtful choices. Too often, however, it is a disorganized series of reactions to what someone else, usually opposing counsel, has done. In order to make rational choices, you should look at a particular negotiation as a whole; get a sense of the wide range of choices you need to make, when you need to make them, and how your choices at one stage affect other stages. Just as importantly, you should know when to choose to not do what is normally done.

This book describes such a systematic approach to negotiation. The same approach should apply regardless of the relationship between the parties and regardless of the subject matter of the negotiation. This book describes an approach to negotiation that asks you, as the lawyer, to step back from the negotiation process and ask, "What stages do I normally go through in a negotiation?" By analyzing the stages a negotiation typically goes through, you can study and practice those stages, thus improving your skills in the area. In other words, this book provides a framework within which to view negotiation. This approach also allows you to plan and implement effective negotiating techniques.

The approach serves as an organizational tool allowing you to simplify a complex process sufficiently to view it as a whole. Just as there is no one way to examine a witness in court, there is no one correct way to negotiate a particular transaction or dispute. An approach for the "typical" examination in trial practice, however, is helpful as an organizing tool. In examining a witness, a useful approach is to (1) introduce the witness (accredit), (2) set the scene, (3) develop the facts either chronologically or topically, (4) anticipate any negative testimony, and (5) end on a high point for your client. This simple approach provides a way to structure an examination, however, which is not rigid, and which must yield to the realities of a particular case.

The approach suggested here serves the same function. We will, for example, identify "ice breaking" as an important stage in the negotiation process. A series of choices relate to this stage, based on the need to develop the appropriate relationship with the person with whom you are negotiating. It would be foolish to suggest that the only time you worry about this relationship issue is at the beginning of a face-to-face exchange. The approach suggests you should do it then, but it also suggests that you should be looking for other opportunities to accomplish the goals of this particular stage.

The skills used in negotiation are part of the broader interpersonal skills many people already possess. You should therefore find some of the material here quite familiar. In addition to developing additional skills, the new material here should help you to develop existing skills more fully. Finally, this book will focus on lawyers negotiating as lawyers. The book, however, will be of value for any setting in which you negotiate.

Chapter 1

NEGOTIATING STRATEGIES AND STYLES

Many authors have attempted to describe negotiation in one all inclusive theory. For example, academics in the forties, fifties, and sixties began using game theory and other mathematical models to describe behavior during a negotiation.[1] More recent approaches include an economic theory of negotiation[2] and social-psychological theories of negotiation.[3] These two theories each suggest different strategies to take in the negotiation.

While a full discussion of these theories is beyond the scope of this book, you should realize that on a practical level these theories suggest that there are two general approaches (and combinations of these approaches) that are used in negotiation. The game and economic theories view negotiation as an adversarial zero-sum process. As its name indicates, the problem-solving theory views negotiation as a problem solving "win-win" process. This book's approach to negotiation combines these two theories, suggesting that while an adversarial strategy is appropriate in some circumstances, a problem-solving strategy may be appropriate in others.

A. Adversarial Negotiation — An Economic Theory and Strategy of Negotiation

Under the economic theory, you can picture every negotiation as involving one or more fungible or interchangeable items, such as money, and the negotiation can be represented in graphic terms. The item being negotiated, damages, for example, is placed on a continuum. If we take negotiating over the settlement of a medical malpractice action, the continuum starts with the physician's insurer paying nothing and moves to an infinite number of dollars. The plaintiff and defendant each make a decision about where they will begin negotiating along this continuum—their opening position. They each will choose a place along that continuum beyond which they will not go—their bottom line

---

1. See, e.g., J. Von Neumann & O. Morgenstern, *Theory of Games and Economic Behavior* (1944).
2. See, e.g., J. Cross, *Economics of Bargaining* (1969).
3. See, e.g., D. Druckman, *Negotiations: Social Psychological Perspectives* (1977).

(sometimes referred to as a commitment point, resistance point, or walk away point).

The area between each side's opening point and bottom line is referred to as their "bargaining range." In the malpractice example, a settlement range exists where the plaintiff's bargaining range overlaps with the defendant's bargaining range. By definition, any settlement that occurs will be within this settlement range.

With the only issue being payment of damages, the negotiation continuum might be pictured as follows:

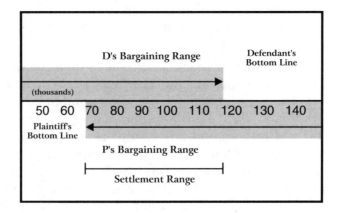

Under this scenario, any settlement will be between $70,000 and $120,000.

Viewing negotiation in this manner has several practical advantages and suggests certain basic elements of the negotiating process. First, this graphic approach suggests that early in any negotiation you must determinee your own bottom line. Second, the graph suggests that you spend much of your time in a negotiation trying to determine the other side's bottom line. While this may seem obvious, what is not obvious, and what the graph suggests, is that your bottom line is the result of rational decision making. Likewise, if your bottom line is rationally based, then a working assumption should be that your opponent's bottom line is also rationally based. If this is the case, you should spend much of the negotiation seeking information that will allow you to recreate the other side's decision-making perspective and, hopefully, their bottom line. As we will discuss later, when seeking information from the other side, you should seek economic, psychological, and social relationship information about the opponent and his or her client that led to a particular bottom line.

This zero-sum or adversarial approach, however, has obvious disadvantages. It suggests negotiation is a contest in which participants stake out positions and then go through a process of concession and compromise. This adversarial model also suggests that there is a winner and a loser. For example, if one side gains a dollar, the other side loses a dollar.

This adversarial approach may well be contrary to the goodwill you are trying to maintain or develop in a particular negotiation. For example, if you are negotiating a peaceful merger of two hospitals, such an adversarial approach may doom the negotiations before they even begin.

This approach also does not consider the fluid nature of negotiation. For example, it assumes that a negotiator determines a bottom line early in the negotiation and sticks to it. In reality, of course, the negotiator's view of an acceptable solution to the negotiation may change as he or she gets more information from the other parties to the negotiation.

B. Problem Solving Negotiation as a Strategy

A second theory views negotiation from a problem-solving perspective. Under this theory, the negotiators are engaged in joint problem-solving. Problem solvers, just as adversarials, are certainly interested in their own needs, interests, and desires. True problem solvers, however, are just as interested in the other party's needs, interests, and desires. As such, problem solvers eschew positions and seek to have the parties openly express these needs, interests, and desires so that the parties may jointly create an appropriate solution to the issue being negotiated. Problem solvers see the "position" of the adversarial negotiator as only one of many solutions to the underlying problem.

A primary advantage to problem-solving is that by addressing the underlying needs of the parties (i.e., the reason behind the position) other, perhaps more creative solutions can be developed. Lawyers have used creative problem-solving in a number of contexts, often to the point where the approach has become institutionalized within a segment of the profession. One such example is in medical malpractice actions. For years, plaintiff's lawyers would demand a set amount of money, such as one million dollars. Defense counsel would offer, if anything, a lower amount. The parties would then move toward some middle ground by a series of concessions and compromises. This was classic adversarial negotiation.

Lawyers, however, have begun using problem-solving approaches, asking, for example, what underlies the plaintiff's need to have one million dollars? If they could identify those needs and solve them, it might cost less money. For example, if the plaintiff claims he needs the money to insure long-term medical treatment, to educate his children, and to compensate for lost wages and the like, the insurer can structure a payment schedule that guarantees these things. The ultimate cost under this structure may be far less than the plaintiff's adversarial demand and can afford a variety of payment methods other than a single lump-sum payment. Hence, structured settlements have become more popular.

There are numerous examples of common uses of problem-solving strategies. Some joint child custody arrangements are essentially problem-solving solutions. Rather than a negotiation premised on dividing time between parents, many parties are asking how to create a living arrangement that accommodates all parties' legitimate needs.

The power of creative problem-solving is particularly evident in situations where adversarial negotiation might lead to deadlock. Remember that for adversarial negotiators to agree, their bargaining ranges must overlap. If the ranges do not overlap, adversarial negotiators will not reach settlement. Take a non-legal example. In the late 1970s, mortgage interest rates were in the upper teens. The banking industry's negotiation with the borrowing public had been basically adversarial, and business suffered. In that negotiation with the public, the industry staked out a bottom line position of 17-18 percent on home mortgages. The public's bottom line, however, was somewhere near 12 percent. The bargaining ranges did not overlap:

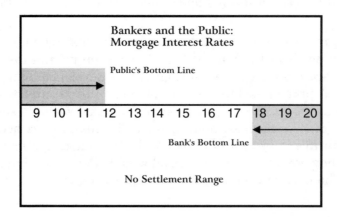

4

The above graph clearly illustrates that if the parties remained adversarial, they could not agree. The banking industry, however, switched strategies. Rather than continuing adversarial negotiation, banks asked themselves what was underlying the customer's position? What were the needs, interests, and desires that led to the position that the public would only pay 12 percent? If the customer's underlying needs, interests, and desires could be discovered, then perhaps some solution other than 12 percent or 17 percent might be appropriate.

Of course, banks quickly recognized that the customer's position was based on his or her inability to pay the higher rate. Further, customers feared that even if they could afford 17 percent, rates could soon fall and he or she would be stuck with a 17 percent mortgage. The industry set about trying to meet its own needs—lend money to make money—and the public's need for affordable payments and protection from being stuck with a high interest rate. The banking industry, of course, came up with adjustable rate mortgages, giving lower payments and protection against falling interest rates.

Lawyers can use the same techniques in more mundane negotiations as well. In property settlement negotiations associated with divorce, it might be that both parties want the same object, for example, a china cabinet. If there is only one cabinet, adversarials are going to have a problem reaching an agreement if each sticks to his or her position that he or she gets it. A problem solver, however, will explore why each side wants the item. If one side wants it because of a perceived inequity in who is already getting the most out of the property, and the other wants it because it is a family heirloom, then giving it to one and compensating the other person with other property may break deadlock. Indeed, problem solvers may find that the reason each wants it is to keep the other from having it! If that is the case, a number of solutions present themselves, including selling it and splitting the proceeds, giving it to the children, or giving it to charity.

In addition to creating multiple solutions, an advantage to problem-solving is that it is generally more conciliatory. The atmosphere is usually, though not always, more cooperative and, therefore, perhaps more protective of long-term relationships.

The biggest drawback to problem-solving is basically one of trust. A premise of problem-solving is that each side must be able to express their needs, interests, and desires. Problem solvers must generally share more information than adversarials. The needs, interests, and desires that are the working material for a problem solver may be the type of information an adversarial fears will weaken his or her position. An adversarial negotiator attempting to avoid disclosure of information might consider revealing underlying needs, interests, and desires as a mistake. Indeed, in a situation where you are a problem solver and the other side is a clear adversarial negotiator there is a real risk. The risk is that the problem solver will reveal information valuable to the other side in assessing solutions acceptable to the problem solver without correspondingly revealing the same type of information about themselves.

Take, for example, the common experience of buying an automobile. In the past, when you bought a car you offered a certain price (took a certain position) and the salesperson immediately took another position. You would make concessions and compromise until you reached a middle ground—classic adversarial negotiation. Today it is more common for you to take a position, "I'll give you $15,000 for the car," and have the salesperson come back and take what appears to be a problem-solving approach by asking, "What were you looking for in a monthly payment?" This is a classic problem-solving question. The salesperson has assumed, usually correctly, that the price you quoted was your perceived solution to your underlying need, that is, the need for a car you can afford. This, of course, is the risk of problem-solving. If you tell the salesperson that your position is based on your ability to pay only $300, the "problem-solving" salesperson can think of all kinds of ways to solve that problem without selling you the car for $15,000. For example, he or she can sell it to you for $18,000 and extend the term of the loan from 36 months to 48 months. This "problem-solving" is done, of course, without the salesperson sharing the equivalent information from his or her perspective. You, the customer, do not get to find out such information as what the car cost the dealer, whether the salesperson needs this car to earn a bonus or increase a monthly commission, whether the dealer is getting any factory incentives, or any other information that you could use to help decide if the dealer would take a lower price.

C. Styles of Negotiation

Besides the two general approaches to negotiation we have referred to as strategy, researchers have identified two styles that are commonly seen in negotiation: competitive and cooperative.[4] Competitive negotiators are aggressive and assertive, and the pitch, pace, tone, and volume of their voices will reflect that style. Cooperative negotiators have a correspondingly different approach. Cooperative negotiators, as

---

4. G. Williams, *Effective Negotiation and Settlement* (1981).

the term reflects, are cooperative in approach, and the pitch, pace, tone, and volume of their voices will be controlled accordingly.

Recognizing that there are two extremes of both strategies and styles begins to suggest the range of possible combinations that you can take in a negotiation. Competitive adversarials tend to be rigid and demanding. Cooperative adversarials tend to view the negotiation process as a series of concessions and compromise. Competitive problem solvers tend to be careful and engage in limited problem-solving, often hesitant to reveal too much information because of lack of trust. Cooperative problem solvers tend to be open and trusting.

Statistically, nothing indicates that one type of negotiator is more likely to be successful than any other. As discussed earlier, however, there are specific advantages to each. A particular negotiator may be naturally more cooperative, albeit adversarial, with an opposing counsel he or she works with regularly, while being a competitive adversarial with the lawyer he or she meets for the first time.

Many people intuitively move from one combination of style and strategy to another. For example, you may have experienced a frustrating negotiation apparently not going anywhere when someone finally said something like "[EXPLETIVE DELETED] I can't stand this! What is it you really want out of this deal?" That person has moved from being a cooperative adversarial to a competitive adversarial to a competitive problem solver.

D. Blending Strategies and Styles

This book takes the approach that both the adversarial strategy and the problem-solving strategy have distinct advantages, and, as with all aspects of negotiation, a choice should be made whether a particular negotiation should proceed from an adversarial perspective or a problem-solving perspective. Indeed, a choice should be made whether you should move from one approach to the other within the same negotiation. As with many aspects of negotiation, we intuitively make such moves. However, you will become a better negotiator by *choosing* to make the moves.

PROBLEM 1.1

Plaintiff, Margaret Polisi, is an attorney who has sued her former law firm, Parker & Gould, and a partner in the firm, Simon Clark. She alleges she was denied partnership in the law firm because she terminated a sexual relationship with Clark. She is seeking compensatory damages in excess of one million dollars. Discovery is complete and the case is set for trial. Lawyers have agreed to meet to discuss possible settlement.

Would you use an adversarial or problem-solving strategy in this negotiation?

Would you use a competitive or cooperative style?

Is there any additional information you need before you can answer these questions?

There is, of course, no one correct answer to these questions regarding representation of Ms. Polisi. The problem is designed to start you thinking about the multitude of issues related to selection of an appropriate strategy or style. Looking at the strategy decision, an adversarial approach might work. After all, according to the complaint, you are dealing with a fungible item—money. To the extent plaintiff gets more, defendants have less. The risk of such an approach, however, is that if defense counsel takes an adversarial approach also, and their bargaining range does not overlap with plaintiff's, the parties may not agree. For example, if defendants want to pay no more than $75,000, but plaintiff has decided she will accept no less than $250,000, there will be no agreement. Your decision to take an adversarial approach, therefore, must be premised, at least in part, on your confident expectation that the opposing side's bargaining range will overlap your bargaining range.

Also, if you represent the plaintiff, does the one million dollars sought in the complaint adequately represent what your client wants out of the lawsuit? Through counseling have you determined that the dollar amount is less important than other intangible issues such as reputation, or feelings of anger, or humiliation? Is the real issue not a fungible item at all? Or, does the client really want a combination of both money and social and psychological vindication? If the client's goals lean toward the latter, then you should take a creative problem-solving approach.

Of course, by starting out as a problem solver, implying "there is more at stake than money," the plaintiff's attorney incurs two risks: revealing important information about the relative importance of money, and not getting as much money in the final deal. You might, therefore, start off as an adversarial negotiator, stake out a position, and then, using the techniques described in the chapters that follow gather sufficient information to determine if the defendant is willing to make a concession. If this strategy does not work, you might then shift to problem-solving. You might accomplish this shift to problem solver by saying:

> *PLAINTIFF'S ATTORNEY: Look, this doesn't appear to be working. Let me tell you, I need a break on this dollar amount. My client has to live until she gets a job with comparable earning potential. And let's be frank, there is no way that $100,000 sends the message that your clients are truly sorry about what occurred. Now I understand you can't break the firm, but let's see if there is some way to meet our client's needs as well as yours. What do you think? Is there some way this remorse can be communicated?*

This example clearly communicates the need underlying the monetary position and invites a problem-solving approach in return. In response, defense counsel might offer to apologize. At that point, as plaintiff's counsel, you should pursue other solutions of this type, move on to other issues, or even return to the money issue by saying something like:

> *Well that's a step in the right direction, but the dollar amount is still too low.*

Of course, in a specific negotiation none of these scenarios may turn out to be the case. The point is, however, that whatever scenario unfolds it may be worth exploring the possibility of a creative, problem-solving solution.

The issue of style requires equally complex decisions. As a professional your immediate reaction may be to cooperate. After all, law has become a business and there is nothing to make you competitive. Indeed, long-term relationship issues may exist, at least for the lawyers. Are these lawyers you deal with on a regular basis? Do you rely on a good relationship to the benefit of your respective clients? If yes, the negotiation will naturally take on a cooperative tone.

The point is simply that you must consider the circumstances of the particular negotiation and consciously select the strategy and style best suited to the situation. Also, as with most choices you make, these choices need not—indeed, often should not—be immutable. As circumstances change, so might your strategy or style. One can easily imagine situations where you might want to start out as a competitive, aggressive individual. Imagine a situation where you represent a child in a short-term state psychiatric facility (average stay six weeks). You discover that your client, an emotionally disturbed 13 year old in the custody of social services, has been in this institution for two years. Your experts tell you that the child could function in a group home, and that, clearly contrary to state and federal law, the child has not been receiving an appropriate educational program.

In these circumstances, you could choose from either of two quite different courses. You could easily conclude that the long-term interests of this child require serious cooperative problem-solving by the very people who have apparently been ignoring the child for at least the past two years. Alternatively, you could just as easily conclude that trying to cooperate and problem solve with people who have callously disregarded the child will be ineffective. You might, therefore, decide that the best approach is to start out as a competitive adversarial— threatening, perhaps even filing a lawsuit, calling for a meeting of lawyers and interested social service and educational providers, and communicating that you are angry and prepared to go to the mat for a client that has been ignored in the past. At some point, however, you would probably have to shift into a problem-solving approach to encourage the relevant service providers to think of creative ways to get the client the services he needs.

Now that we have discussed the various strategies and styles of negotiators, the next chapter will introduce the various stages of a negotiation.

Chapter 2

THE TEN STAGE NEGOTIATION

A. Phases and Stages

Regardless of the strategy or style used, theorists tell us that each negotiation is made up of three phases: assessment, exchange, and persuasion.[5] Each of these phases, in turn, involves a number of discrete tasks. Assessment, for example, involves among other things, acquiring information and evaluating what it means in terms of your goals and the likely goals of the person with whom you are negotiating. The exchange phase typically involves acquiring more information, disclosing information, and presenting a position or proposed solutions. In the persuasion phase, the parties attempt to convince each other to accept a particular proposal. These phases clearly overlap. For example, acquiring information is central to the negotiating process, and cuts across each of the phases.

The approach suggested here takes these phases and associated tasks and breaks the negotiation process into ten interrelated stages. These stages are roughly, though not always, chronological. Just as the three phases overlap, these stages overlap as well. If you think about the last negotiation you engaged in you can probably identify each of these stages. We will address each of the stages in detail in the chapters that follow, but for now a brief overview is helpful.

---

5. R. Bastrass & J. Harbaugh, *Interviewing, Counseling, and Negotiation* (1990).

Ten Stage Negotiation

Preparation and planning

Ice breaking

Agenda control

Information bargaining

Proposals, offers, demands

Persuasion/Justification

Concessions/Reformulation

Crisis: resolution or deadlock

Closing

Memorialization

The first stage of any negotiation is *preparation and planning*. Whether you prepare for hours or only as a disgruntled colleague walks into your office, most people give some thought to an upcoming negotiation. In the preface it was pointed out that choice is critical to success in negotiation. Maximizing preparation and planning will increase your ability to anticipate the choices that need to be made.

Having done as much preparation as circumstances allow, the next stage involves some type of interpersonal contact, or *ice breaking*. The amount of time spent on ice breaking may vary, but it virtually always occurs.

The third stage involves *agenda setting*. Fairly early in the process, there will be an agreement on what is subject to negotiation. Are you there, for example, to discuss a merger, settlement of a defamation action, the terms of pre-trial stipulations, or jury instructions? As importantly, however, at this stage you should be concerned with establishing how you will negotiate. For example, how will you get the negotiation to move through these ten stages in the order you want them?

Following a discussion of the purpose of the negotiation, there is typically an exchange of information, often referred to as *information bargaining*. During this stage you will seek information, reveal information, and even hide information from each other.

After information bargaining there typically follows a series of stages involving persuasion and exchange. One party makes a *proposal, offer*, or *demand* and then provides a *persuasive statement* or *justification* of why the proposal, offer, or demand should be acceptable to the other side. This process will repeat itself and *counter proposals, offers,* or *demands* may be presented, also followed by a persuasive statement or justification. *Concessions* (if you are an adversarial negotiator) or *reformulation of the proposals* (if you are a problem solver) then may follow until ultimately a *crisis* occurs; the point at which the parties either agree or break off discussions. Then there follows a *closing* and the agreement or lack of agreement is then *memorialized* in some manner, usually in writing.

To reemphasize the comments in the preface, you must recognize that this is not an inflexible framework. In fact, viewing negotiation as a series of stages is useful only if it is flexible. This framework's value is that it lays out in a straightforward manner the myriad choices that we must make in a negotiation. Once we understand that a face-to-face negotiation generally proceeds through these stages, we can then alter it in a given circumstance, even combining stages.

Agenda setting is a good illustration of why this framework is only roughly chronological. The parties may have set the agenda by letter before the initial personal contact. Or, in a negligence action when plaintiff and defense counsel sit down to talk, both already know that the agenda will include duty, breach, causation, and damages.

As another example, an important stage in the negotiation is the exchange of information. Although first in importance, it is not the first stage in a face-to-face negotiation. Many other things must occur first. In a given negotiation, however, you will choose to move the information exchange stage or major parts of it because of circumstances unique to that particular negotiation.

In a negligence action, serious negotiations to settle the case may not take place until after extensive formal and informal discovery. Counsel will obtain most of the historical facts of the action before the formal negotiation. Indeed, to wait until the face-to-face negotiation would be incompetency at its worst. But some information may be available only in the setting of settlement negotiations, such as given the state of the suit at this particular time, and what are the real needs of the parties, economically, socially, and psychologically?

B. A Note on Plea Bargaining

Two types of plea bargaining take place in criminal proceedings. First, charge bargaining involves, as its name implies, negotiating over the crimes with which the defendant will be charged. Prosecutors have a wide range of crimes (burglary, grand larceny, breaking and entering, etc.) with which to charge a defendant found outside a home at night with a stereo in his hands. Charge bargaining involves negotiating which of these the prosecutor will charge the defendant, and to which he ultimately pleads guilty. Second, sentence bargaining involves negotiating the sentence the prosecution will recommend the defendant receive in exchange for a guilty plea.

Within each of these types there will often be issues unrelated to either the specific crime charged or the sentence that will be received. For example, in negotiating a recommended sentence, the defendant may have authorized defense counsel to trade his testimony against a co-conspirator.

Recent statutory developments have made charge bargaining increasingly important. Mandatory minimum sentences and other sentencing guidelines often leave little discretion to the prosecutor if the focus is on sentence reduction.

Does any of this discussion of the stages of negotiation apply to plea bargaining? Yes. Prosecutors and defense counsel have the same variety of styles as do civil attorneys. Plea bargainers experience the same stages of the negotiating process as other negotiators. Criminal attorneys must prepare and plan. Prosecutors must choose the appropriate relationship with opposing counsel. Both negotiators agree on an agenda. Acquiring information concerning the strength of the prosecution's case is just as important to criminal defense counsel as the strength of plaintiff's case is to civil defense counsel.

Also, prosecutors and defense counsel come in various combinations of styles and strategies. Some defense counsel, for example, will be adversarial, staking out a position and viewing the process as a series of concessions and compromises: "My guy didn't do it and you can't prove it, but he wants to get this over with so he'll agree to the misdemeanor charge." Defense counsel are also just as likely to be problem solvers: "Look, he's just a kid and needs help. The real problem is not that he shoplifted the goods; it's that he doesn't have the home structure he needs. How about we hold the charges and see if we can't get him into . . . ."

There are, however, a number of factors that affect the plea bargaining process in a way that do not always affect transactional or civil litigation disputes. Two factors, for example, significantly affect information bargaining in plea negotiations. First, favoring the prosecution, is the fact that it has the resources of the state at its disposal. While clearly the state does not always choose to overwhelm the defendant with these resources, the fact remains that the state, if it so chooses, can outspend almost all defendants. Second, favoring the defendant, is that, in most jurisdictions, discovery in criminal actions clearly favors the defendant, with the prosecutor having a greater responsibility for turning over evidence than the defendant.

With this general overview we will now turn to a detailed discussion of each of the stages. As we discuss each stage, keep in mind that we will want to identify not only what we need to do, but how we do it. We also want to ask ourselves whether how we do it differs depending on which style and strategy we use.

Chapter 3

THE SOCIAL PSYCHOLOGY
OF NEGOTIATION

Researchers have long recognized that a social/psychological dynamic permeates all stages of the negotiation process. This "social psychology" can have a significant impact on the negotiation. Our own personal observations confirm the fact that people do things in a negotiation for reasons other than a rational business or economic judgment. If you can identify these potential pressures, you can then use them to help "persuade" the person with whom you are negotiating to accept your proposal. As importantly, if you recognize these "other pressures" at work on you, you can choose to either allow yourself to be influenced by them or to choose to not let them influence the negotiation.

Social psychological pressures occur in a variety of circumstances. We are all familiar with situations where a person has taken a position that can only be justified by their desire to "save face." With perhaps more worthy motivations you may recall situations where you or another person in the negotiation "gave" the other side a concession because they "wanted to be nice," or "to avoid a fight." The lawyer who agrees to a day off for a member of the staff because she likes the staff member may have an economic motivation (keeping a good employee happy), but the lawyer also may just feel good by waiving a policy that might otherwise prohibit the day off.

Organizations are also subject to social psychological pressures. We sometimes read in the newspapers about the social and psychological aspects of major negotiations. One need only read about a bank, or any other business merger, in which the two entities are going to combine names, or create an entirely new name. Certainly combining the two names may have an economic justification—taking advantage of name recognition—but people involved in these types of negotiations will also tell you that combining names provides a soothing compromise for people with an emotional attachment to the original name.

A PRACTICAL GUIDE TO NEGOTIATION

A review of some of the more common social psychological influences will illustrate how these pressures work to facilitate or inhibit acceptance of an opponent's particular position.[6]

A. Audiences to the Negotiation

Researchers point out that an audience can significantly impact a negotiation. By "audience," we do not mean simply that someone may be in the room watching the negotiation. By audience it is meant that someone somewhere is observing directly or indirectly the negotiation or its results.

The types of audiences are quite broad. They run from the obvious—a colleague sitting in on the negotiation—to the more subtle—your spouse when you discuss your day at the office. Audiences to a negotiation involving a lawyer include, for example:

- the lawyer's supervisors or superiors;
- the lawyer's professional peers, colleagues, co-workers;
- the lawyer's spouse;
- the current client in whose interest the lawyer is negotiating;
- other clients;
- potential clients.

Psychologists tell us that the existence of an audience motivates negotiators to seek positive evaluations from the audience. This is common sense. No one wants to go back to the office and reveal to his or her colleagues that they have just made the worst agreement of the year.

Of course, different audiences will evaluate a negotiation differently. A supervising partner may evaluate the associate-bargainer from a profitability (to the firm) and quality standpoint. Did the lawyer get a good deal in a difficult negotiation? The client might evaluate the bargainer in light of factors such as speed or profitability to them (as opposed to the firm). The one common denominator, however, is that if the negotiator is accountable to an audience, this accountability provides a means to control the negotiator.

---

6. One of the most complete analyses of the social psychology of negotiation is Rubin and Brown. In *The Social Psychology of Bargaining and Negotiation* (Academic Press 1975), these two authors catalog a wide variety of documented psychological considerations. See also D. Druckman, *Negotiations: Social Psychological Perspectives* (1977).

In blunt terms, if you can give the negotiator what an influential audience desires, you can manipulate the lawyer to accept what the audience wants, as opposed to perhaps what the lawyer wants. The clearest example of this, of course, is the client as audience. In our defamation action for Ms. Polisi, we will spend a great deal of time trying to figure out what the audience/client really wants. If you can figure out what the client wants, more likely than not, the desires of the lawyer with whom you are negotiating become irrelevant. Give the lawyer what the client wants and the lawyer should ultimately go along.

PROBLEM 3.1

Refer to Problem 1.1, where plaintiff's lawyer is negotiating with defendant, the law firm Parker & Gould. Plaintiff alleges both sexual harassment and defamation.

What audiences would there be for the negotiation?

How, if at all, would your overall strategy of the negotiation be affected by those audiences?

Is there any additional information you need before you can definitely answer these questions?

The client is not the only audience. For example, in Problem 3.1 defendants Parker & Gould have an audience that consists of other law firms. If plaintiff, Polisi, can identify how Parker & Gould views that audience, plaintiff's attorney can use that information to advantage. For example, is the existence of the lawsuit generally known in the legal community? If not, the threat of continuing the suit and risking exposure with a resultant loss of prestige may have considerable influence on the negotiation and Parker & Gould's willingness to settle. If the existence of the suit is already generally known, this knowledge could conceivably make settlement harder. For example, the defendants may feel that to settle the case will have a significantly negative impact on the firm's reputation if a settlement is interpreted as an admission of liability. The reputation of the firm may be better served by going to trial and suffering a defeat than to admit responsibility. Putting together an acceptable settlement package under these circumstances will be particularly difficult if plaintiff's own goals include seeking precisely the kind of public recognition of liability that Parker & Gould seeks to avoid.[7]

As with all aspects of the negotiation process, the pressure of an audience must also be evaluated from the negotiator's perspective. The negotiator who has the audience must try to avoid being manipulated by that audience. For example, a common question for lawyers is whether the client should attend the actual face-to-face negotiation with the opposing counsel. As with most issues related to negotiation, there is no one right answer. This audience dynamic, however, is certainly an important consideration in deciding whether the client should be present.

In a negotiation involving a business transaction that requires a high level of technical expertise, there is often little question that having a client with that expertise attend could be of assistance. The value of that expertise must, however, be weighed against the fact that opposing counsel will have direct access to your most important audience. If the client is unable to control his or her reactions to opposing counsel's negotiation ploys, you may be at a serious disadvantage.

It should be quickly added that the cooperative problem solver must be as aware of these dynamics as the competitive adversarial. For example, lawyers are constantly subject to scrutiny by colleagues. Human nature being what it is, the lawyer probably prefers to be respected by his or her colleagues as opposed to being held in low esteem. If the general wisdom among opposing counsel's colleagues values aggressive negotiations, the lawyer likely will behave accordingly. Recognizing this, the competitive adversarial should take steps to avoid exacerbating that characteristic. The cooperative problem-solving defense attorney should probably try to avoid plea bargaining with the competitive adversarial prosecutor in the hallways of the court where other prosecutors or police officers are present.

---

7. We intuitively recognize the power of manipulating people through use of an audience in many everyday transactions. Anyone who has ever been a disgruntled customer who seeks to speak directly to a supervisor recognizes the power of going to the audience/ultimate decision maker. Anyone who during the negotiation to buy a car has asked to speak to the sales manager is likewise seeking access to the all important audience.

B. Restraints on Communication

Researchers also tell us that restrictions on communication can have a significant impact on the negotiation. These restrictions may be either between the negotiators or between the negotiator and the negotiator's own people. For example, communication isolation imposes constraints on the development of cooperation and promotes distrust and suspicion. A party who is unable to contact her own support group (colleagues, supervisor, secretary) may be more distrustful.

The lesson seems obvious that if you are dealing with a person who is generally distrustful to begin with when trying to work out a joint venture, it may be to your advantage to ensure that this type of isolation does not occur. You might propose meeting at the other lawyer's or other client's place of business. Or, if you meet at your office, try to ensure your counterpart has frequent opportunities to take breaks and use the telephone privately.

PROBLEM 3.2

Assume you are a lawyer for Margaret Polisi in the sexual harassment and defamation action mentioned in Problem 1.1. You wish to set up a meeting to discuss possible settlement with counsel for Parker & Gould. You have now called three times leaving messages. The attorney for Parker & Gould has returned your calls twice, but you have been out of the office.

How is Parker & Gould's attorney likely to feel?

How would you feel under these circumstances?

What steps might you take to deal with the communication problem?

Does the communication problem give you any insight into other aspects of the negotiation?

Restrictions on verbal communication between negotiators also can have a negative impact on the process. When verbal communication is eliminated effectiveness often suffers. All too frequently this occurs when you play telephone tag with someone. As your frustration develops over your inability to contact a lawyer, your anxiety or anger may increase, making it less likely that you will develop the relationship necessary to complete the deal. It may seem obvious, but using a letter at this point can be extremely helpful. Likewise, voice mail is underutilized as a means not just of leaving a message requesting a call in return, but actually to engage in a discussion by leaving a detailed message outlining needs, interests, and the like. Leaving a message that the lawyer should return your call at a specific time when you will be in your office, can be very effective.

Keep in mind that if you feel frustration and anger, the other person may be feeling it as well. Directly confronting this may help maintain or develop an appropriate relationship.

C. Social Psychology of Selected Tactics

Many standard negotiating techniques have psychological overtones. Several of the more common are worth addressing here.

1. Timing Ploys

A common negotiating technique is to set a deadline by which agreement must be met. This tactic often works. As time pressures increase, bargaining aspirations, demands, and the amount of bluffing tends to decrease.

2. Overly Demanding

Some research has shown that perceptions of one side being demanding, resisting, or unjust, correlates with the other side raising intangible issues of honor, public image, face, and self-esteem.

PROBLEM 3.3

You are in negotiations with the city concerning its treatment of panhandlers. The city has begun a public crackdown on such behavior. Your clients, however, believe that the city has overstepped constitutional limitations. Your only goal is to get the city to change the policy.

What overall strategy should you use in this negotiation?

What style should you use?

In some circumstances, you must be careful not to come on "too strong," particularly where the expected response from those with whom you are negotiating is that they fear a public loss of status or control. Under these circumstances, the opposing negotiator may make a "strategic" decision that regardless of the ultimate outcome, he or she must make a public show of opposition in order to maintain that public perception.

How this will play out depends on the specific circumstances. For example, assume you are negotiating with the city concerning its treatment of panhandlers. If your only goal is to get the city to change the policy, the above described dynamic suggests that people be brought into the process privately and early on, before filing a lawsuit, with sufficient opportunity to listen to their input and to allow the public to see them as cooperative team players. Problem-solving will be at a premium.

Your client, however, may have other goals in mind besides changing the city's behavior in this specific instance. If the client wants to expose a pattern of behavior, you might make public demands while recognizing that in the short term it will make the city more likely to resist. As with everything associated with negotiation, no one right way exists; there are only choices given the circumstances of the particular negotiation. Also, your history with the city might be such that you know that regardless of which approach you take, the city will react aggressively and that ultimately you will have "to go public" to put additional pressure on the city. It all depends.

3. Deference Toward Authority

In general human interaction, bargainers display considerable deference toward high, or higher, status people by frequent compliance with their threats and by submissive behavior. For example, if you as a supervisor meet a subordinate in the cafeteria and say you would like to meet at 3:00 p.m., the employee likely will come to your office at 3:00 p.m. He or she will have deferred to a higher authority.

PROBLEM 3.4

What steps in your position at work can you take to establish that you are the higher authority?

Many different things create the authority or the impression of authority that can work in response to Problem 3.4. As you look around your practice setting, what things indicate authority or lack of authority? Titles clearly do. Bankers have long recognized the importance of titles and use the title of vice president quite liberally to create the impression of authority. Are such titles present in your work environment? Compare the title of staff attorney versus associate general counsel.

Physical environment can also create the impression of authority. Do you negotiate in a cubicle or in a formal conference room? Two very different impressions can result. Similarly, dress can help establish authority. Why do physicians wear white coats in the hospital even when not performing clinical roles? Status and authority are communicated.

Perhaps most importantly, what does your negotiating behavior say about your authority? Do you need a supervising attorney to approve every action? Has an agreement you have reached been re-evaluated by a supervisor, who then required that you seek changes?

4. Extreme Demands

In negotiations that reach agreement, bargainers generally attain higher and more satisfactory outcomes when they begin with extreme rather than more moderate demands. This makes sense when you recognize that one of the primary problems associated with negotiation is not having sufficient information to know the strength of your position. When you buy a car you usually do not have sufficient information to know whether your offer is too high or too low. Anyone who has bought a house knows the fear of the seller accepting your first offer and your own reaction or feeling that if they accepted the first offer it was too high. We will discuss in detail how to avoid this situation through a systematic approach to negotiation. You should always keep in mind that when in doubt, ask for more rather than less.

Of course, a risk is associated with extreme demands. While an extreme demand may result in more if settlement is reached, an extreme demand may increase the perception of a lack of willingness to negotiate seriously and therefore increase the risk of deadlock.

5. Allowing Yourself to Be Persuaded

Another important social/psychological factor at work in negotiations is that a bargainer wants to believe he is capable of shaping the other's behavior—of causing the other to choose as he does. Therefore, you might occasionally want to let it be known that you have been persuaded by the person with whom you are negotiating. This may in turn create a more favorable relationship between the two of you.

6. Promises and Threats

If a bargainer believes he can not successfully exert influence in other ways, he may revert to promises and threats. Threats result quite often from a negotiator's feeling of frustration and inability to develop more constructive approaches. If you supervise other people, think back to when you have had to threaten disciplinary action if the person did not change their behavior. Most likely, the threat was the result of frustration that other, more constructive action failed. When you feel the pressure to threaten, or when you are threatened, your first thought should be that the threat is in reality a warning. The threat is a warning that you should redouble efforts to try to find more constructive actions.

The need to find alternative approaches in the face of threats is critical because the use of threats decreases the likelihood of a mutually favorable result. Once again, this is common sense. When you are threatened, what is your usual response? Are you more likely to give in, or fight on regardless of the cost?

Merely identifying that these things occur is not enough. You must be prepared to identify their likely occurrence in a particular negotiation and plan how to either use them to your advantage or minimize their impact. Take threats, for example. If you believe the person you will negotiate with will likely use threats, and it will negatively impact the negotiation, prepare to respond accordingly. The appropriate response requires you to ask why people make threats. Typically, they make them because they have nothing else to use to get you to comply. Your first step may be to ensure that the negotiation takes a more principled approach, providing a more meaningful way of discussing problems. Your second step is to deal directly with the threat, by asking what would make a threat effective and then diffusing these items. How to do this is discussed in Chapter 7, the Exchange.

D. Gender Differences

Women who negotiate on a regular basis often report that women are treated differently by men in negotiations. Reports that women are subject to more attempts to intimidate them are not uncommon. Women also report that they seem to approach the negotiation differently than men. Is there any truth to these anecdotal reports? Research indicates there may be some truth to these perceptions, though the data are mixed.

Professor Gerald Williams[8] has reported that, based on his empirical research, people do not change their approach to negotiation based on the sex of the opposing party. Men who are cooperative in one setting typically are cooperative in all settings. This does not mean, however, that the perceptions reported by so many women are wrong. What this means, Williams theorizes, is that aggressive individuals are aggressive in all settings. Therefore, some men will make sexually demeaning statements to women, such as "It's a tough world out there, honey, and you better catch up," as a means of intimidation. These are likely the same men who will make intimidating statements to other groups, saying for example, "When you get a little more experience out here, son, you'll learn this is the way we do it."

---

8. Williams, G., *Effective Negotiation and Settlement* 65-67 (National Practice Institute 1981).

On the issue of whether women behave differently in a negotiation, Williams points out that in hundreds of studies on the issue, equal evidence indicates that women behave differently and that they do not. Among those studies that indicate women behave differently, researchers came to the conclusion that females tend to be more cooperative than males.[9] These same researchers have found that woman tend to be initially more trusting.[10] Other researchers have also found that woman sit closer and generally show more cooperative nonverbal communication.[11] Consistent with these findings is a study that shows that the more women act like stereotypical males, the more credibility they will have with men.[12] Again, however, just as many studies indicate there is no difference.

9. Rubin, J. and Brown, B., *The Social Psychology of Bargaining and Negotiation* 172 (Academic Press 1975).
10. *Id.* at 171-173.
11. Harper, R., Wiens, A., & Matarazzo, J., *Nonverbal Communication: The State of the Art* (1978).
12. Cash and Janda, "The Eye of the Beholder," *Psychology Today* 46 (December 1984).

Chapter 4

PREPARING AND PLANNING
FOR THE NEGOTIATION

A. In General

Adequately preparing and planning for the negotiation are crucial to success. However, lawyers frequently fail to give this adequate attention because of competing demands for their time. Good negotiating practice requires that you take whatever time is available to prepare for the negotiation, even if it is only ten minutes between meetings, or ten seconds as you leave your office to talk to a disgruntled staff member.

Obviously, the more time you have, the more you can prepare. Because of discovery, you will frequently have access to a vast array of information about the parties, the events, and the alleged damages well before the face-to-face negotiation begins. In other circumstances you may not even know the name of the person with whom you are negotiating before he or she walks in the office door, such as a prosecutor in a large metropolitan area prosecuting 80 shoplifters a day. Even under this latter set of circumstances, you can effectively prepare if you are aware of the stages that must be completed in all negotiations.

Three broad issues must be dealt with in preparation and planning. First, you must identify what your client seeks to accomplish from the negotiation and what options are available to you to reach those goals. The adversarial negotiator converts those options into a position which he or she seeks to convince the other side to accept. For example, the client identifies, with his lawyer's help, the goal of having an income stream of sufficient size to allow the client to live comfortably despite permanent injuries received in an automobile accident. An infinite number of alternative positions ranging from none to billions of dollars exist on the issue of enough money. The adversarial negotiator working with the client identifies the least advantageous alternative along this continuum that the client is willing to accept (e.g., the least he or she will accept). We typically call this the negotiator's bottom line or walk away price. The adversarial negotiator will then identify an opening position along this continuum as an opening offer or demand.

A problem solver is less likely to stake out either a bottom line or an opening position, but must still identify the client's goals and any potential solutions that will allow these goals to be achieved. For example, a problem-solving lawyer, having identified an income stream as the goal, is likely to see a set amount of money in settlement as merely one possible solution. If providing a certain quality of life is the real goal, lump-sum payments are only one way to meet that goal. Other possibilities are structured settlements or the possibility of money plus training. Rather than immediately focusing on a limited number of positions, the problem solver will begin thinking of numerous alternative ways to achieve the goal.

The second broad issue that you must address in preparation and planning requires you to begin analyzing information to determine what you believe to be the other side's goals and any perceived solutions to meet those goals. The adversarial negotiator asks herself what is the likely position the other side will take, and what is their probable bottom line. The problem solver begins to ask what the other side is likely wanting to achieve and what they will likely see as appropriate ways to achieve that goal. Both types of negotiators must, to accomplish this task, begin assessing the information presently available to them and begin thinking about the additional information they would like to have. To the extent this information is available from sources other than the person with whom you are negotiating, preparation requires acquiring this information.

The third broad task in preparation and planning is to begin deciding how you are going to achieve your goals in the negotiation. The list of decisions can be quite long. The overriding question, however, is quite simple: How can you maximize your success in this negotiation?

If you accept this book's premise—that a systematic approach based on a multi-stage process will allow you to achieve better results—the question then is, what do I do to make my approach effective? At this point we have a bit of a chicken and egg problem since we have not fully identified the stages. It will come as no surprise given the above discussion, that gathering information will be critical. We must ask, therefore, what steps do we take to maximize acquiring information?

B. Determining Your Client's Needs, Interests, and Desires—The Necessity of Effective Client Counseling

Effective client counseling is critical to effective negotiation. For the adversarial negotiator to determine a bottom line or for the problem solver to assess needs and to begin developing alternative solutions to the problem being negotiated presupposes both: 1) that the client has effectively articulated those goals, and 2) with your help has begun to identify acceptable solutions.

Pre-negotiation counseling typically focuses on a process that moves the client toward at least tentative decisions. Whether those decisions relate to the potential terms of a settlement in a personal injury lawsuit or the ultimate structure of a business arrangement in a transactional negotiation, you must have the client work through at least an elementary decision-making model.

Although there are certainly more sophisticated, or at least more complex, decision-making models, for our purposes a relatively simple model will suffice.[13] Whether intuitively or systematically, what we typically do in working with clients who need to make a decision is to first identify their goal. What do they want to get out of the negotiation? Quite often the client has multiple goals and he will need to decide which are critical and which he can live without. In *Polisi v. Parker & Gould*, for example, the plaintiff may have the goals of both returning to the firm and of punishing the firm. If you represent the plaintiff, you must have Ms. Polisi prioritize these goals. She must consider whether the goals are mutually exclusive.

In helping the client identify the goals they seek to achieve, you must be careful to distinguish their goals from their position in the negotiation. Goals tend to be broader aspirations. For example, Ms. Polisi may say her goal is to make Parker & Gould pay her a great deal of money. While this may indeed be a goal, it may also be only a reflection of a position designed to achieve some different, perhaps broader result. After careful discussion you may find that what Ms. Polisi really wants is for Parker & Gould to admit their behavior and be punished in a way that minimizes the likelihood the behavior will occur again. Polisi's desire for a large amount of money is merely one way of achieving the broader goal.

---

13. For a fuller discussion of similar counseling models see R. Bastrass & J. Harbaugh, *Interviewing, Counseling, and Negotiation* (1990) and D. Binder & S. Price, *Legal Interviewing and Counseling* (1977).

After goals have been clarified, you must next help the client identify possible solutions to achieve those goals. The range of possible solutions available to Ms. Polisi are somewhat limited if the goal is to achieve a large cash settlement. She may have considerably more alternatives if punishment is the goal.

As just stated, after you have identified the broad goal, you next begin identifying options which will allow you to meet those goals. If you focus on a cash settlement, you can identify an infinite number of options ranging from zero to billions of dollars. Each of these options will then be viewed in terms of positive and negative consequences.

Certainly one of the most significant types of consequences you can weigh will be the economic consequence of an alternative. Again, take the simple personal injury settlement example where the only issue is dollar amount. You and your client will consider the positive economic consequences of seeking a large settlement: acquiring a large amount of money that will make life comfortable for as long as the client lives. The negative economic consequence of seeking that large settlement may be that first, the demand is unlikely to be successful and second, opposing counsel may not take your position seriously, causing the negotiations to fail before they even get started.

More than economic consequences, however, will be considered. Remember our discussion of the social and psychological dynamic in the negotiation in Chapter 3. These social and psychological pressures affect our decision-making. Therefore, whether intuitively or systematically, you will factor social and psychological consequences into your assessment of the relative merits of options. A positive psychological consequence in seeking the large settlement might be that the client will feel that he or she is finally on the offense, standing tall, and "Not taking it any more." A negative psychological consequence may be that given the unlikely acceptance by the other side, your client will continue to worry about the lawsuit and its related effects on his or her life. To the extent that the client is being pushed by a spouse, a positive social consequence of the alternative will be that the spouse is not angry with the client's position. On the other hand, a negative social consequence may be that a spouse may be angered by the excessive demand.

Balancing all the consequences—both positive and negative—you and the client will conclude that at some dollar amount, the negatives outweigh the positives. If you adopt an adversarial approach, your search for a bottom line or walk away position ends when you find this point. In our example, it may be that the positive consequences of accepting $50,000 outweigh the negatives. At $49,999.99 the negatives may outweigh the positives and, therefore, be unacceptable.

The types of consequences affecting a particular negotiation will vary with the circumstances being negotiated. The economic consequences of a particular settlement will vary greatly. You can, however, identify a number of general categories. First is the direct economic payoff of the particular deal. Will the client be financially better off as a result of this agreement? If you are representing a company in the sale of a major asset, your client will consider such items as the cost of production, value of goods, how much the market will bear, desire to cultivate a relationship with the purchaser, availability of other suppliers, storage costs, and alternate dispositions of the asset.

You may also consider collateral economic factors, such as the cost of agreeing or not agreeing to the sale, or whether if you do not work out this deal you will not get other deals. If you do agree to a certain economic solution, consider whether the result, if it becomes general knowledge, will cause the next person you negotiate with to expect the same treatment? How about lost work? Will the cost of getting a particular deal take more time than it is worth?

The social and psychological consequences also will vary from deal to deal, but there are some common types of social relationships that you should consider. Not surprisingly, these are similar to those discussed in Chapter 3. For example, if you have to deal with a person on a social level, it is possible it might impact your decision.

This process is as critical to an adversarial negotiator as it is to a problem-solving negotiator. While the problem solver may not convert options into positions over which debate proceeds during the negotiation, clarifying goals, identifying alternatives, and understanding various consequences are essential for you to develop creative problem-solving solutions.

In a particular negotiation, of course, your options may be more varied than accepting or rejecting a fungible item like money. Indeed, a problem solver is likely to only tentatively fill out such a chart, because the problem solver would expect that as the parties discuss the underlying needs, interests, and desires, they will identify additional options. Still, you may find it useful to begin clarifying the advantages and disadvantages of known options by listing them as shown below for the plaintiff in *Polisi v. Parker & Gould*:

Polisi — Goals and Options

Goals:	Be compensated for economic loss caused by termination and punish firm so that it will not happen again.
Option 1:	Rehire Polisi with credit toward partnership of time since termination, payment of back wages during time of termination, an apology for termination.
Advantages:	Economic damages covered.
	Apology acts as punishment.
Disadvantages:	No guarantee that Polisi won't be fired in the future or that partnership share will not be adversely affected.
	Apology is private and no guarantee that corrective action will be taken.
	It will be an unpleasant place to spend professional career.
Option 2:	Payment of lost wages from date of termination until new employment is found and payment of $100,000 in punitive damages.
Advantages:	Continued receipt of money to carry on search for new meaningful employment.
	$100,000 will make significant economic impact on firm to encourage corrective action, while at same time making client feel good about the result because of clear vindication.
Disadvantages:	Lost "equity" in credit toward partnership at a prestigious law firm.
	Vindication is essentially private and money does not guarantee corrective action.

C. Anticipate Other Side's Bargaining Range

Having identified your client's goals, you must next assess the other side's probable position. Here, as in other parts of the negotiation process, it is useful to place yourself in the position of the other side. If you have gone through a decision-making process described in the previous section, it is possible the other side has as well. As such, you should assess the available information to judge the likely goals the other side may have, as well as the options they are likely to have identified as meeting these goals. You then should start assessing the information available to you to determine the consequences that are perceived by the other side. What information do you have available to you to determine their likely positive and negative economic, social, and psychological consequences?

Having assessed the available information, the next logical step is to determine what additional information you need and how you can get access to the information. A lot of information is, of course, available through formal and informal discovery. Where information is obtainable only from the other side, you must decide how best to acquire that information. For a discussion of acquiring this type of information, see Chapter 6 on Information Bargaining.

An adversarial negotiator will find it useful to view the process of determining the other side's bottom line in light of our adversarial versus problem-solving approaches of negotiation. Take for example, the situation described in *Polisi v. Parker & Gould*. The following diagram illustrates the plaintiff's negotiation plan:

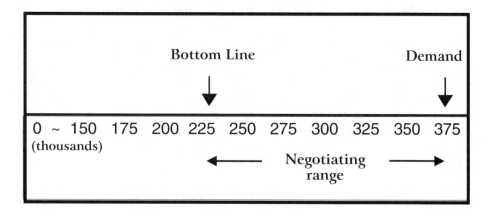

The next step for an adversarial negotiator is to begin gathering and assessing information so as to recreate the other side's bargaining range. In a perfect world, with perfect information and an idiot on the other side, adversarial negotiation is a process by which you seek information sufficient to judge the other side's bottom line and then offer it to them. Of course, in the real world there is not perfect information, and all other people are not idiots. In our example, you might assume that the opening position of the other side is that no payment will be made. What you are trying to assess is information that will let you decide how far up the scale the person is willing to go. Because you made your decision based on economic, social, and psychological consequences and their relative importance to you, as an adversarial negotiator you seek the same type of information from the other side to allow you to recreate their decision-making. Graphically it might be presented as follows:

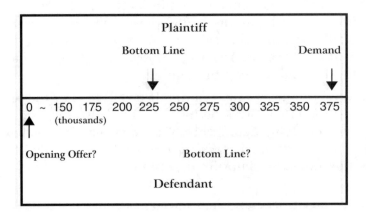

The problem solver is going to seek and assess the same type of information. Rather than seeking the information to fathom a bottom line, the problem solver wants the information so that he or she can determine the needs, interests, and desires that have to be met. If the problem solver can identify these needs, interests, and desires (economic, social, and psychological considerations) they can then begin considering and proposing alternative solutions which will satisfy both sides.

A problem solver will also seek to develop alternative perceptions of the problem in such a way that additional proposals can be created. In *Polisi*, for example, the problem solver will recognize that plaintiff's demand for $250,000 is merely their proposed solution to what plaintiff sees as an underlying problem. The problem solver will try to determine the needs, interests, and desires that underlie the position and attempt to jointly formulate a solution that meets those needs, interests, and desires. The problem solver in proposing a solution may well end up rejecting a narrow definition of the issue as how much money will be paid, and reformulate the issue to: "How do we ensure Ms. Polisi's uninterrupted professional development?"

A problem solver will use this approach in a wide variety of circumstances. Assume you are negotiating with a bank on behalf of a business client who is trying to avoid bankruptcy. The bank, quite predictably, may have expressed increasing discomfort with the loan. As a result of the bank's perceived (indeed very real) increased risk the bank seeks to increase the rate on a line of credit. The adversarial negotiator from the bank will determine the level of risk the bank faces, and equating rate with level of risk, determine the minimum rate acceptable to cover the risk while simultaneously trying to determine the maximum rate the customer is likely to pay. The problem-solving lawyer might try to recharacterize the negotiation and seek information about the bank's underlying concerns while trying to explain past failures on the part of the client.

This may result in finding that the underlying business is quite good, but that the customer is unable to exercise competent fiscal management and has a lousy accounting system. The problem solver might also find out that these are the bank's expertise. While the rate may go up, the problem solver might be able to minimize the rate increase by agreeing to "purchase" services from the bank that work toward solving the underlying business problem.

D. Planning to Implement the Negotiation Process

Once you have assessed existing information concerning the other side's position, you must next address a third area of preparation and planning: What steps should be planned and taken to maximize the success of the systematic framework we are trying to implement? Any number of process issues exist. How will you set the agenda? How will you ask questions? When will you make your first offer? Other questions arise that relate to specific stages in the process. Let's look at a few of these issues.

1. Your Place or Theirs

Where should you conduct the negotiation? This question is instructive because it illustrates that a systematic approach may lead you to a conclusion that is contrary to popular wisdom. Many books on negotiation will tell you to always have the person come to your turf. It creates a psychological advantage for you; they have already made a concession and it puts you in the "power position." Such a rule is, however, inconsistent with the premise of this book—choice is critical.

You may get a psychological advantage by negotiating in your office. If you concentrate on the issue of information gathering, however, you will see that the answer is not so clear. Ask yourself, "If information is critical, where am I likely to get the most information, my office or theirs?" Looking at it simply as a question of where information is stored, you will likely get more information at their place. Viewing their surroundings will give you a great deal of information both about the substance of the negotiation and the other side's personality. A lawyer's visit to a potential business partner will give that lawyer information about that person or business just from the physical surroundings.

If you want documentary information, going to their office may also make more sense, since they will have a harder time saying, "Gee, I don't have that with me," than if they were in your office. On perhaps a bit more sophisticated level, people are generally more comfortable on their own turf. As comfort goes up people are generally more willing to talk. Since the more they talk the more information you get, it once again may make sense to meet in their office.

You have to choose, given the particular negotiation, which place is better. In fact, you may decide a third location or the telephone is best. There may be considerations that lead you to negotiate by phone despite some of its obvious disadvantages, such as loss of nonverbal communication and access to other information. If, for example, you are intimidated by the other person, the telephone allows you to place distance between you and that person and to hide your own insecurity.

The above discussion assumes that you are able to control location. In certain circumstances your only choice will be between doing the negotiation at one location or not negotiating. When your boss calls, you will probably meet wherever the boss wants to meet. Similarly, telephone negotiation is often required because of practical considerations of time and distance. Your only choice is between using the telephone or not negotiating.

Of course, even with an issue as straightforward as where the negotiation is to take place we have more than one consideration.

Information, although important, is not everything, and you must consider other factors. Among other factors that make negotiating at your place an advantage are:

- your ultimate authority source may be easier to contact;
- avoiding the inconvenience of being removed from other obligations;
- the psychological advantage that the other side came to you;
- saving money and travel time;
- managing atmosphere, including being able to control interruptions.

On the other hand, additional advantages of going to their site include:

- concentrating fully on the interaction;
- the other side must deal with interruptions;
- easily leaving someone's office, rather than asking someone to leave yours;
- communicating a willingness to work with the individual by going to the trouble of visiting them.

2. Determining a Purpose/Developing an Agenda

How are you going to control the negotiation process? Beyond getting information, you need to ask how much information do you need and what kind of information do you seek? A particular meeting, for example, may simply be a get-acquainted meeting where the emphasis will be on developing a relationship. Acquiring information relevant to a particular agreement might be secondary. On the other hand, the meeting may be one in which you chose to seek as much information as possible about the other side so that you can prepare a detailed proposal to submit at a later time. What you expect to get should in part determine how you structure the negotiation session.

You can also plan how you are going to obtain the information. Are you going to use open-ended questions or narrow questions? Will you proceed to the point of asking for precise pieces of information, or will you stick to generalities at this stage?

3. Determining Personal Attributes to Take

You can plan what your style is going to be during the negotiation. We change our personality quite often in unconscious ways. We often act differently at home than at work. Our personality with a superior may be significantly different than with a co-worker. To some extent we make these changes consciously and we should to the extent that it fosters our goals. We can choose to be cooperative or adversarial depending on what we are seeking. You can be open about your feelings or closed. You can communicate a structured approach to interviewing or an unstructured approach. The possibilities are limitless. Here, as with all aspects of the interpersonal process, the idea is to *choose* to act in a certain manner for a specific purpose.

Related to personality traits is the idea that you are able to plan to play or not play certain roles. Society often defines certain roles for individuals and you should decide whether playing that role is to your advantage. We know that a lawyer with a large firm in a major metropolitan area may have a public perception quite different from a solo practitioner in a rural area. Whether these roles or stereotypes are accurate or not, you can decide whether to fit into that stereotype. A particular person you are negotiating with may react favorably to it, whereas a client may not.

4. Planning the Setting

The setting of the negotiation is often something that you can plan. We have already discussed location, but if the negotiation is going to take place at your location, you should think about the physical setting. As will be discussed in more detail in Chapter 6, nonverbal communication can impact the session. Furniture arrangement may facilitate or inhibit the exchange of information. Research suggests that people seek some barrier, but not too great a barrier between themselves and the person they are talking to.

Applying research such as this, a lawyer sitting behind a desk with the opposing lawyer sitting directly across may get less information than if the two sit around a low coffee table. Some psychologists would also say that the absence of any barrier can inhibit communication. The feeling that you are invading the "space" of the other person may increase their anxiety level to a point where it inhibits communication.

If resources permit, plan the setting to meet some happy medium and have sufficient flexibility to allow for differing personalities you may interview. The common setup of a sofa and chair at right angles allows the person to position herself at a comfortable distance from the other negotiator. Something as simple as having chairs with wheels may allow you the needed flexibility.

5. Choosing a Strategy

Another important planning question is whether you are going to be an adversarial negotiator, problem solver, or some mix of the two? Will you be competitive, cooperative, or something in between? You should also begin to anticipate the other side's probable strategies. Are they likely to be adversarial negotiators or problem solvers? You should develop intermediate positions short of your bottom line and be able to justify each of those positions. If you are willing to offer a prospective associate an annual salary of $45,000, would you prefer $40,000? If so, should you start by offering $35,000? Given what you know about this person, will offering less hurt the long-term relationship?

You should also investigate any controlling principles and determine whether they must or should be followed. Your ability to negotiate may be restricted by statutes, regulations, or rules of professional responsibility. Often you can question conventions that may apply. If you are selling a major asset, purchasers may expect you to set the price. A convention in most purchase and sale settings is that the seller sets the price. You might like to avoid doing this, at least early on, since price always depends on the other side's needs and you might want more time to assess these needs.

PROBLEM 4.1

Assume you are hiring a new staff member to work in your law office.

What conventions, or controlling principles, are there that you should be aware of?

How might you change these expected conventions?

In the above problem, a convention often at work in the employment setting is that, not surprisingly, the employer sets the salary. If you are hiring someone, you might want to reject this convention if you have insufficient information as to the appropriate salary. You may already do this intuitively if you have ever asked someone what their salary needs are. Prospective employers also commonly ask for a salary history before the interview takes place. Both of these actions are ways to change a controlling convention that an employer makes the first offer on salary.

6. Plan Use of Extra-Negotiation Factors

Plan the use of extra-negotiation factors. Can regulators, insurers, or others be helpful? For more details, see the discussion in Chapter 8 on alternate dispute resolution.

7. Everything Else

These implementation issues are examples of the many parts of a negotiation that you must plan. In the chapters that follow as we identify what we need to do to implement the negotiation, we will simultaneously identify additional areas that require preparation and planning. It may be obvious, but it is still worth saying: If you have to do something in a negotiation, you have to plan how you are going to do it. Thorough preparation requires you to go through each stage of the negotiation and ask, what do I need to do, and how am I going to do it?

Chapter 5

OPENING DISCUSSIONS:
ICE BREAKING AND SETTING THE AGENDA

A. Ice Breaking

At the beginning of virtually any interpersonal communication, the participants engage in a process of ice breaking. This stage typically involves small talk about non-threatening topics. Every good negotiation should allow appropriate time for this to take place. Ice breaking serves several important purposes. Primarily, this stage focuses on developing an appropriate relationship with the other side. Small talk at the beginning of the negotiation places the other person more at ease, and as the comfort level increases, the willingness to provide information should increase.

Ice breaking also provides an opportunity for you, the lawyer, to put yourself at ease. Your anxiety level may be higher than normal and if you start talking about non-threatening topics it should help decrease your anxiety.

You should not overlook the opportunity to gather information during ice breaking. This provides you a good opportunity to gather information with which you can evaluate the other side, view their personality traits, and decide whether you can work with them. Also, ice breaking is a good opportunity for the other side to evaluate you. When you refer to a picture of children on the desk of the person with whom you are negotiating, and that person responds, "Yeah, she's a cute kid, but then that's not why we're here," you have received important information about that person's future conduct and desire to set up a pattern of interaction.

How much time is necessary for ice breaking is a reflection of many things. Perhaps the most important of these factors are: 1) prior relationship with the person; 2) available time; and 3) other person's inclination. For a long-term relationship the ice breaking at a particular meeting may be short or even non-existent. This may merely be a reflection of the fact that ice breaking has been going on for years and the goals associated with it have been met. A new relationship will normally require more time to allow both you and the other person to meet the goals.

Typically, people naturally fall into some type of ice breaking or small talk. Too often, however, ice breaking is ineffective in terms of our goals because it proceeds along the following lines:

> LAWYER 1 (L1): Ms. Jones, thanks for coming in today. Did you have any trouble finding the office?
>
> LAWYER 2 (L2): Oh, no, not at all.
>
> L1: Good. I know parking can be kind of difficult around here, especially in the rain.
>
> L2: Yes, I can't believe this weather.
>
> L1: So, how can I help you?

Perhaps the biggest problem with this type of exchange is the topic. These topics are so obviously ice breaking that the participants never get beyond a stilted "obligatory" exchange that merely provides a transition to the important part of the negotiation. It is the equivalent of the statement, "How are you doing?" as you pass a colleague in the hall. Each knows the other is not at that time really interested in a response to the substance of the question.

To effectively meet our goals for ice breaking, the discussion must proceed more naturally, covering topics that do not invite a reaction that this is a mere formality. Having this type of discussion is obviously easier with someone with whom you already have an established relationship. The relationship gives you a common background of information which allows you to pick a topic you can feel comfortable with and that will be both non-threatening and interesting. A person who has a family can be asked, "How is John doing at college?"

The goal for situations without a preexisting relationship is to evaluate the information available, however limited, and to see if you can find a non-threatening topic to discuss. When visiting a person's place of business this is much easier because your presence at the location will give you information. A set of golf clubs or picture of a sailboat on the wall provide ample opening for a discussion related to those activities.

Even the person that comes to your office has provided at least some information from which you can glean a topic. If the person is from a supply company you might simply state, "I was interested when I heard that you were connected with the XYZ firm. I've always had an interest in ___." Even a person without an appointment brings the fact that they are unannounced and a good humored, "This is what I like about the job, tell me how did you decide on me?" might be appropriate. Or, you might choose to be more competitive and put the person on the defensive by saying something like, "I suppose I can make some time available now."

If we view the negotiation as a series of interrelated steps, we can ask whether any of the other steps can be facilitated by ice breaking. Ice breaking also provides an opportunity to gather important information in its own right. In other words, an appropriate topic for ice breaking can also produce important information. For example, a general question of "How's business?" if answered may give you important information about time, importance of the subject of negotiation, etc.

PROBLEM 5.1

Assume counsel is negotiating with a lawyer that has flown in from a distant city. Counsel have scheduled an early morning meeting. The following occurs:

> *LAWYER 1 (L1): Hello, Mr./Ms. _____.*
> *Nice to meet you. How was the flight over?*
>
> *LAWYER 2 (L2): Fine.*
>
> *L1: Did you just get in?*
>
> *L2: Yes.*
>
> *L1: Did you have time to check into the hotel yet?*
>
> *L2: No.*
>
> *L1: Would you like my secretary to call and confirm for you?*
>
> *L2: No, not really. Actually I was hoping to wrap this up and get on the road to catch a flight.*
>
> *L1: Great. When does your flight leave?*
>
> *L2: In about two hours.*

What are the advantages of such an exchange?

In Problem 5.1, the first lawyer picked a topic that is appropriate for developing the appropriate rapport with the person. Ensuring their comfort communicates concern for them as individuals and allows them to talk, helping put them at ease. The topic also provides important information that there is a time constraint, and that the other lawyer is confident that a resolution will be reached in fairly short order.

This example also illustrates how the approach must be flexible. Having struck upon this important point, the lawyer might alter the framework, jumping to information bargaining to follow-up on this topic. The lawyer continued to ask questions, making sure that she understood the extent of the time constraint. The lawyer, however, should remember to return to complete the ice breaking and agenda setting.

In addition to gathering information, ice breaking provides an opportunity to begin setting the overall strategy and style of the negotiation. In the above example, the lawyer is clearly setting up a cooperative style. A competitive style could as easily be set by cutting ice breaking short or showing a lack of interest in the other person as an individual. Just as you can begin to set the style, you can evaluate the style of the other side during ice breaking.

Problem 5.1 also gives you a sense of the evaluation process that can go on. Even from the bare transcript, it appears other lawyers may not be responsive to extended ice breaking. The short, yes-no answers may be communicating impatience with a process that is not "all business."

B. Agenda Control: What and How You Will Negotiate

At some point, the parties should agree on an agenda for the negotiation. Absent a surprise visit or telephone call, part of the agenda is typically set before the interpersonal contact takes place. In other words, the parties are almost always aware of *what* they are going to negotiate. The parties may have previously set the agenda by phone, mail, the complaint, indictment, or the like. Even then, however, someone is likely to say as a transition from ice breaking, "Well, I guess we're here to discuss *Polisi* (or the merger/the contract/or the like)." There may also be additions to the agenda based on information you have acquired: "Thanks for sending me that information. I know we set this meeting up to talk about . . . , but as I went through the information, it looked like maybe we should talk a bit about . . . . Given what I've seen here, they may help us save some money and give you a better position."

In certain circumstances, what you are to negotiate may well constitute a separate negotiation. On the international level, this can be seen where countries conduct preliminary negotiations before summit meetings on the topics the leaders will actually discuss at the summit. This also occurs in legal contexts. In a merger or acquisition negotiation the parties may disagree over whether a basic issue is even negotiable. Where the parties sit down to discuss merging personnel policies, the acquiring business may be in such a strong position that it insists that whether the acquired business changes its policy is not a negotiable issue, but only when it will do so. Likewise in many (most?) plea negotiations, guilt on at least some criminal charge is a given.

As important as agreeing on what to negotiate, is *how* you are to negotiate the issues. Research indicates a correlation between success and ability to control how the negotiation proceeds. This makes sense if you accept the fact that a systematic approach to negotiation results in better settlements. If, as we will discuss, information bargaining must precede making an offer, then the party who ensures that it can information bargain before being forced to make a proposal will likely do better.

Saying you need to control the agenda is one thing, but how do you do it? Perhaps the most obvious way to try to gain control is to simply begin the negotiation the way you want to and assert control. Using the ten step process, start ice breaking, state your agenda, and then start information bargaining, as in the following example:

> *LAWYER 1 (L1): That sounds like a great vacation. You must have had fun.*
>
> *ANSWER (A): We sure did.*
>
> *L1: Well, we better get down to business. I know you are busy, so I don't want to take up any more time than necessary. I have found that the best way to proceed is if we first make sure we're here to talk about the same thing—the possibility of my client exchanging his testimony against Smith in exchange for a deal on the liquor store charge.*
>
> *A: That's right.*
>
> *L1: Good. Then let's do this. I'd like to ask you some questions. Find out a bit about your perspective. After I have had a chance to do that, you can ask me some*

questions. After I've had a chance to get to know your needs better, then I'll be in a position to see if there is anything we can work out.

Note in this example, defense counsel has basically said that she is: 1) going to set the agenda; 2) going to information bargain; and 3) only then consider whether a proposal is appropriate. This approach helps you deal with the person who attempts to get you to commit to an offer before you have had a chance to discover important information. You can use the same approach for deciding which issues to negotiate. You might approach an angry lawyer as follows:

LAWYER 1 (L1): Mr. Smith, Carol tells me there is a problem. Please come to my office.

LAWYER 2 (L2): I can't believe it!

L1: Can I get you some coffee?

L2: No. You can tell me why my client's got ten years seniority and ends up getting fired while on vacation. This is unacceptable!

L1: I see you are quite angry. Let's talk about it. Tell me what you see as what happened and let's see if we can figure out a way to get your client to understand what has happened and why.

In this example, the lawyer attempted through ice breaking to set a more reasonable tone, as well as to suggest that a problem-solving procedure is appropriate. At the same time, the lawyer has suggested that the issue to be negotiated is to explain to opposing counsel's client what has happened and why. What the lawyer is trying to keep off the agenda is changing the employment decision.

Controlling the agenda, however, is more than trying to ensure that the process goes through these steps. If you want to be a problem solver, it means setting the style and keeping it set.

L1: Charlie, our clients have been working together a long time. And, I hear your client wants to reconsider their arrangement; deviate from the terms of the contract. Let's do this. You tell me where your client sees itself in the next few years, what its goals, plans, and desires are. Then let's see how we might meet those needs.

Controlling the agenda also involves ensuring that where multiple issues are to be discussed, you control the order in which you discuss the issues. For example, you may want to start with a minor issue. You might concede the issue and then set up a fairness doctrine, that it is now the other person's turn to give something. Negotiating the minor issue might also allow you to: 1) establish competence to negotiate; 2) test the other side's preparation; or 3) develop a pattern and practice of agreement.

Controlling the agenda also means recognizing that you can characterize or quantify an issue in a number of ways, and seek to have the favorable characterization accepted. Take as an example the sale of a large asset. When the lawyer negotiates with a potential buyer, the actual price can be set using a number of values: depreciation, appreciation, return of investment, need to get rid of the asset, need of the customer to have the asset, appraised value, or some combination of these. Effective agenda control means getting the discussion to proceed using the valuation method most favorable to you, or at least getting the most using the valuation system the other side prefers. The effective negotiator will be prepared to argue the appropriateness of each such characterization and may even be able to show how several of these methods arrive at the same favorable result.

Preliminaries to a negotiation are frequently lost opportunities to lay the groundwork for a successful setting. The above discussion has shown how you can use even the small-talk at the start of a negotiation to your advantage, and how to set and control the agenda. We will next turn to the important information gathering phase of a negotiation.

Chapter 6

INFORMATION BARGAINING

Having established the agenda, the negotiation typically moves into an exchange of information stage. This stage of the negotiation requires you to ask yourself: 1) what information do you need to seek; 2) what information do you want to disclose; and 3) what information do you want to hide? Your decisions on these three questions will significantly impact the negotiation's outcome.

PROBLEM 6.1

Given what you know about the distinction between problem-solving and adversarial negotiation can you think of any general distinctions between the two approaches when it comes to deciding what to seek, reveal, or hide?

We will not discuss Problem 6.1 at this point. As you read through this chapter, however, see what distinctions there are.

A. What Information Do You Want to Seek?

The adversarial negotiator wants to obtain information that will allow her to determine the other side's bottom line. As we discussed in preparation and planning, the adversarial negotiator seeks to identify information that will allow a reasonable estimate regarding that person's bottom line.

The problem solver wants to have information so that he can determine the needs, interests, and desires to be met. If these needs, interests, and desires can be identified, the problem solver is in a position to begin considering and proposing alternative solutions that satisfy both sides.

The range of useful information, of course, depends on the issues being negotiated, though they tend to fall into economic, social, and psychological considerations. For example, in *Polisi v. Parker & Gould*, defendants would like to know what the job market is like for someone with Polisi's qualifications, whether Polisi is able to sustain herself during protracted litigation, and what her long-range plans are. In the areas of social and psychological considerations there are a number of participant-related factors based on the social psychology of the negotiation process as discussed in Chapter 3. Among these factors are:

Negotiator experience

Although statistical evidence shows that experience alone does not make you a good negotiator, lack of experience may mean you have deficiencies which the other side can exploit, such as lack of confidence or lack of understanding the value of a particular negotiating chip being discussed.

Your own common experience will without doubt confirm this. People new to a job are generally less confident. Statements made to this person, such as, "Well, the way we usually handle this is . . . ." can increase this discomfort. When you were new to your job you may have felt that way. Less experienced people that you deal with probably feel that way as well.

PROBLEM 6.2

Assume you are a prosecutor getting ready to meet with a public defender who has just passed the bar. You are going to discuss the possibility of the public defender's client pleading guilty.

> **How might an adversarial negotiator use the inexperience of the person they are negotiating with to their advantage?**
>
> **How might an adversarial treat this inexperience differently?**
>
> **Is there a risk to negotiating with an inexperienced negotiator?**
>
> **If you are the one that is inexperienced what might you do when dealing with an experienced negotiator?**

Looking at the questions raised in Problem 6.2, an adversarial might decide to exploit the possible inexperience by highlighting her own experience. Occasional use of phrases such as, "Your predecessor always did this," or "As you get more experience, you will see that we usually do it this way," may increase insecurity. This insecurity may in turn create a willingness to concede when in doubt.

The problem solver, on the other hand, might view inexperience as an opportunity to educate the other person, persuading them that there is a better approach than staking out positions. Statements such as, "I've found the best way to approach these negotiations is to ____," may be effective.

The risk of an inexperienced negotiator on the other side is that insecurity does not equate to trust, and trust is what is ultimately required. At some point the adversarial is going to offer her bottom line, and they will want the other person to believe it is true. If the negotiator is not at their bottom line, then further concessions may have to be made because they were not believed. Even worse, if the negotiator is at their bottom line, there may be no agreement because the other person thinks there is more to be conceded.

Lack of trust is a risk for the problem solver as well as the adversarial. The problem solver will need to persuade the other side that problem-solving is appropriate and that ultimately a given proposal is the best for everyone concerned.

Another risk is that the inexperienced negotiator will have precisely the opposite reaction to that anticipated. That is to say, their reaction may be: "I'm new to this and I'd better show I'm tough." Indeed, the social-psychological pressures discussed in Chapter 3 may very well force the inexperienced person to protect herself by being less accommodating.

From the perspective of the inexperienced negotiator, as with any tactic that is used against you, you have to communicate that the attempt to use your inexperience against you will not be effective. This might mean you respond to statements that, "This is the way it is usually done," with the simple statement, "I'll check that out when I get back to the office." When dealing with particularly heavy handed attempts by your opponent to play-up their experience, you may choose to confront the problem directly: "Let's get serious Charlie, I know you have more experience, but that's not going to get you any place."

Time constraints

Research indicates that time pressure tends to increase the likelihood of agreement because bargainers reduce their aspirations, demands, and bluffs. This suggests that when you believe the other side is making excessive demands or is inappropriately trying to bluff you, you might try setting a time limit. When dealing with such a person, simply limiting the time you give them can often be effective: "Charlie, I'm glad we were able to meet. Unfortunately, I'm pressed today and I've got to be at another meeting in fifteen minutes."

Authority to settle

Does the other negotiator have the authority to settle and what are the limits of that authority? When you make a proposal, you need to persuade the other side. Who must you persuade; the person you are dealing with or someone else? If it is someone else, then you need to know this so you can find out what is important to the decision-maker.

Anyone who has bought a car knows how effective it can be to separate the negotiator from the person with the real authority. Anytime the salesperson is confronted with an offer from you, they take the offer to the sales manager. Not surprisingly, the salesperson usually comes back saying the sales manager said no. You ask why, and you get a very ambiguous, "It's just not good enough." You then ask to talk to the sales manager, and the salesperson says that is not possible. If this happens, you should probably walk out. How can you effectively negotiate if you cannot find out what the real decision maker values?

PROBLEM 6.3

It is easy to overestimate the value of separating yourself from the ultimate authority. While there may be advantage to the ability to make statements such as, "I'll have to check on that with my people," what are the disadvantages?

The biggest disadvantage in separating yourself from your authority is illustrated by your reaction when the tactic is used against you. A normal reaction is, why aren't you negotiating with the person with authority? Or worse, it may be seen as a bald attempt to manipulate you. Finally, such tactics can seriously affect your credibility. If you constantly refer to a higher authority, your own statements may be less credible: "Why should I believe you now, when on other important issues you said you had to check with your boss?" Likewise, repeated references to a need to check with someone else will often result in repeated pressure by the other side to speak directly to that authority.

Work load of other side

Is the other negotiator so overworked that they have an incentive to resolve the matter quickly?

Who and how paid

Does the other negotiator get a direct reward for this negotiation, and if so, how is it determined? Is the attorney on the staff of the entity or person he represents, or has he been hired on an hourly basis? Is there a motivation to resolve the matter quickly to avoid additional expense? If you are negotiating with a salesperson, are they on commission? Can you find out whether the commission is based strictly on individual sales or does the commission depend on when the sale takes place. For example, salespeople sometimes earn a higher commission for a certain level of total sales within a period, such as a quarter. Would your particular sale move the salesperson up to a higher commission?

Motivation or desire to be a problem solver or an adversarial

We have discussed how the strategy the parties choose can affect the nature of the negotiation. Which strategy is the other negotiator likely to take: adversarial, problem-solving, or some combination of the two?

B. Where to Get Information

Having decided what information you want, the question then becomes how to gather the information. First, you should remember that because of its critical role, valuable information should be obtained from anywhere, at any time, from any source. One value of viewing the negotiation process as a series of interrelated stages is that while emphasizing that certain things are done at certain points in the negotiation, it also suggests that fruitful opportunities to meet the goals of one stage may present themselves in other stages. Ice breaking is a perfect example of a stage where you can facilitate information bargaining. Topics that might be appropriate to discuss during ice breaking may well be inappropriate at a later time.

Imagine that you have to schedule a negotiation session. It is summer time and you either call the person or see them at some social function. You might take the opportunity to work on the relationship, while also gathering some important information. The conversation might go like this:

> *LAWYER 1 (L1): Charlie, it's good to see you. I'm sorry I haven't gotten back to you. Your call came in while I was on vacation.*
>
> *CHARLIE: Did you have a good time?*
>
> *L1: Great time. Went to the beach. Back now and ready to go. How about you? Any vacation plans?*
>
> *CHARLIE: Yes. We're taking the family to the beach ourselves.*

L1: Great. Where do you go?

CHARLIE: Got a place down on Long Beach. Spend a couple weeks each year down there. Sort of a family tradition. My folks come down. We have a real good time.

L1: Sounds like fun. When you heading out?

CHARLIE: Week from Friday.

In this brief interchange, the lawyer has discovered information that can be used to facilitate the negotiation. The adversarial negotiator might use this information to schedule the negotiation just before the planned vacation, based upon the theory that Charlie would probably want this resolved before vacation so that it does not worry him during vacation. The problem solver, however, might use this information to set the appropriate relationship and to develop trust by saying, "Well, let's not let our business interfere with your trip. What would be best for you, meeting before or after your vacation?"

In addition to deciding where to get information, you should consider the wide number of sources of information. Sources of information can be categorized as either indirect or direct and as verbal or nonverbal.

An indirect source is any source other than the person with whom you are negotiating. A wide range of possible sources exist, depending on the particular negotiation. The lawyer going to opposing counsel's office indirectly can gain valuable information by viewing the office. In *Polisi v. Parker & Gould,* the plaintiff's lawyer may be able to find out information about how highly Parker & Gould values its reputation by asking other lawyers or law firms. Periodicals as common as the daily newspaper may contain financial information about the firm.

Certain information must, of necessity, be obtained indirectly. Take the purchase of a car. Perhaps the most important piece of information that a car purchaser can have is the car's actual cost to the dealer. Once the purchaser knows this, they are in a much stronger position to make an offer. You will probably not get this information directly from the car dealer, but you can obtain it from an indirect source such as one of the many consumer-oriented magazines or books.

Direct methods involve gathering information directly from the person with whom you are negotiating. The most obvious direct source are the statements made by the person with whom you are negotiating.

Documentary material, of course, can be just as critical in many negotiation situations.

C. How to Get Information in General

In the context of the give and take of negotiation, you cannot underestimate the importance of gathering information face-to-face. The most common way to get the information is to ask for it. The techniques used to ask for information during a negotiation are fundamentally the same as those used whenever the goal is to acquire information.

D. Types of Questions

As with negotiation in general, information bargaining can be more effective if it is approached systematically. To develop a systematic approach to asking appropriate questions in a negotiation, an understanding of the various types of questions is necessary.[14]

One way to categorize questions is by who selects the topic of the question, the questioner, or the questioned. In general, questions categorized in this way are of four types: open ended, narrow, yes/no, and leading. Which type of question you ask should result in different information being given, both in terms of quantity and quality of information. As with most aspects of interpersonal skills, there is no one correct type of question to ask. Each type of question has its own advantages and disadvantages. By looking at these various advantages and disadvantages, however, you can derive some general principles or suggestions for appropriate questioning.

1. Open Ended Questions

An open ended question allows the person questioned to select the topic and to discuss what she believes is important about that topic. A classic open ended question, thus, would be, "Tell me, what's on your mind?" or, "Can you tell me about your plans?"

---

14. An excellent, detailed examination of question formation, upon which much of this discussion is based is found in R. Gorden, *Interviewing: Strategy, Tactics and Techniques* (4th ed. 1987). A number of other texts have adopted this useful terminology. See, e.g., R. Bastrass & J. Harbaugh, *Interviewing, Counseling, and Negotiation* (1990) and D. Binder & S. Price, *Legal Interviewing and Counseling* (1977).

The advantages of open ended questions are several. First, and perhaps most importantly, open ended questions normally get you the most information. The person questioned is urged to talk about whatever is of concern, without restrictions concerning topic or limitations as to length of response. When combined with good active listening skills (discussed below), the open ended question maximizes acquisition of information.

Because the person is encouraged to talk, open ended questions also will normally increase the likelihood that a good rapport will develop between the negotiators. The fact that you are willing to listen should communicate your interest and your understanding, thus allowing you to more effectively develop a good working relationship with the other person.

Another major advantage of open ended questions is that they encourage the other person to identify the important agenda items. Whenever you are negotiating with someone you will usually have a list of topics that you feel are important and need to be explored. If you use an open ended question before you turn to your own topics, you will increase the possibility that you will find out what is important to the other person. You can then compare what is important to you and what is important to the other person and structure further questions accordingly.

Getting the other person to raise topics can be particularly helpful if you need to explore sensitive items. For example, if you are trying to negotiate the agreement to merge two companies, the scenario might work out as follows:

LAWYER 1(L1): Let's talk about your needs.

ANSWER (A): Well, they haven't changed much since we last talked. Independence is still critical. The support you folks can provide our company doesn't outweigh the inconvenience of an extra administrative layer we don't want. Central administrations can be lousy in the best of circumstances.

L1: Anything else?

A: Well, to be honest, we need to protect the senior management.

L1: What else?

To the extent that the senior staff is a problem, the other person has raised the issue and at some time it may make it easier for the lawyer to come back and say, "You mentioned the senior staff. Tell me more."

PROBLEM 6.4

Imagine you are going to interview a person to find out as much about their employment as possible.

Imagine you are limited to asking questions that can be answered yes or no, what questions would you ask? What would you anticipate to be the difficulties of this task?

Now imagine you can ask any questions you like, what questions would you ask?

Problem 6.4 provides a useful exercise illustrating the importance of open ended questions. Take 60 seconds and interview someone about their employment using only questions that can be answered yes or no. The exchange might go something like this:

Q: Do you fix things?

A: No.

Q: Do you make things?

A: No.

Q: Do you provide a service?

A: Yes.

Q: Are you a doctor?

A: No.

Q: Are you a banker?

A: No.

Q: Are you a dentist?

A: No.

Q: Are you a lawyer?

A: Yes.

Q: Do you do criminal work?

A: No.

Q: Do you do civil litigation?

A: No.

Q: Do you do transactional work?

A: No.

The number of questions could go on forever, and you might not get the information you need. Yes or no questions require you to think of every possible piece of information that may be important; a task that is impossible for most people. In this interview example, you need to be able to conceive of every possible variation on employment to be sure that you have all the information. Even when you get a yes for an answer the task simply presents an infinite number of new questions:

Q: Are you employed?

A: Yes.

Q: Have you been employed for more than a year?

A: Yes.

Q: Have you been employed for more than two years in your current job?

A: Yes.

The logical approach, of course, is to ask an open ended question. Not only will you get more information, you may get information you would never have thought to ask about. Ask your partner open ended questions and what is likely to happen?

Q: Tell me about your job, would you?

A: Well, I'm a law professor at the University of Richmond School of Law, and have been for the past 16 years.

Q: Tell me more.

Nonetheless, open ended questions also present several disadvantages. Because the person will be free to discuss anything, you may get a higher amount of irrelevant information. The level of irrelevant information may be particularly high if the person has brought any psychological needs such as venting anger. The irrelevant information may also be so great that the person's response becomes unduly long and diffuse. On the other hand, this time and effort may pay off in the form of a better rapport. Further, it should be obvious that we only know the information is irrelevant after hearing it. In the midst of a great deal of irrelevant information you may also find one important piece of information. A final disadvantage to open ended questions is that being general in nature, they allow the person answering more flexibility in avoiding questions. As a result, you may need to follow up with more direct questions.

2. Narrow Questions

A narrow question is a question in which the questioner selects the general subject matter and which aspect of the subject matter is to be discussed. For example in our interview example in Problem 6.4, a narrow question would be, "What courses do you teach?" The biggest advantage of this type of question is that because it is more specifically focused, it increases the likelihood that the questioner will only receive relevant information. Assuming the person questioned is cooperative and not seeking to avoid giving information, a narrow question elicits a higher percentage of relevant information in response.

The disadvantage of a narrow question, however, is that the total amount of information received will be less than with an open ended question. Narrow questions provide much less opportunity for the other person to raise topics, and thus, if the questioner does not come up with the topic, the topic may not get raised. All the questioner is likely to receive in response to the previous question is information concerning the other courses taught, whereas in our open ended question we may get additional information. Further, the ability to gather complete information using narrow questions assumes the questioner has sufficient knowledge of all relevant areas of inquiry.

In terms of developing a rapport with the other person, a narrow question may work either as an advantage or a disadvantage. To the person seeking a sympathetic ear, the narrow question provides less opportunity to meet these psychological needs. To lawyers in a hurry, however, the narrow question may be a more efficient use of limited time.

3. Yes/No and Leading Questions

Questions that can be answered yes or no have the advantage of high quality, accurate information (assuming the truthfulness of the person questioned). However, as pointed out with open ended questions, this accuracy comes at the expense of reducing the quantity of information.

Yes/no questions can also be characterized as being direct and consequently are usually more threatening than more open ended questions. To certain people this will harm rapport development, increasing anxiety or communicating a perceived lack of "personal interest" on the part of the person asking the questions.

Finally, leading questions are an extreme form of yes/no questions that suggest the answer to the question. The questioner asks, for example, "You're looking for a settlement structure that provides Ms. Polisi with a stream of income until she can get a new job, right?" As with yes/no questions, assuming the truthfulness of the person questioned, the quality of information is quite high. Leading questions have, however, all of the disadvantages of yes/no questions plus the additional problem that they facilitate your being misled. To the extent that you indicate to the person what an appropriate response is, the quality of information may actually go down because you are hearing what the person believes you want to hear, not necessarily the truth as seen by that person.

E. The Funnel Approach to Questioning

The four types of questions discussed above form a continuum going from open ended to narrow. If we view the advantages of each of the question types, we see that certain questions are appropriate for different circumstances. The good questioner uses each type of question when it is appropriate, given the particular advantages of the individual question type. Indeed, it is possible to view fact gathering as starting at either end of a continuum running from open ended questions and working toward leading questions.

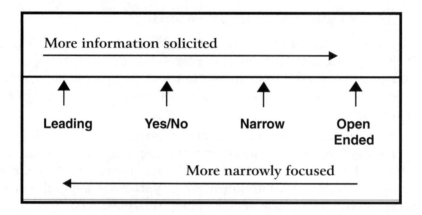

Moving either from leading to open ended or open ended to leading questions, the questioner uses all four types, thus taking advantage of each type of question.

Going from open ended to leading questions is referred to as a funnel approach. As a general rule, most experts recommend that when you seek to systematically gather as much information as possible, you should use a funnel approach.[15]

---

15. See P. Hoffman & D. Malone, *The Effective Deposition* (NITA, 1993) for a discussion of using the funnel approach in depositions.

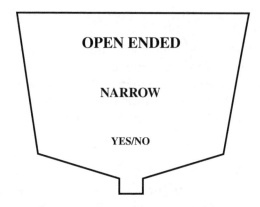

OPEN ENDED

NARROW

YES/NO

Since open ended, general questions help develop rapport and a good relationship is something that you usually seek to have throughout the negotiation, a funnel approach seems most appropriate. If we want to systematically approach information gathering, we need to identify the important topics early in the process. Open ended questions help you to do so. Further, remember that the burden of narrower more specific questions is that the questioner must have first thought of the general topic. To the extent that we want to encourage the other person to suggest information that we ourselves might not cover, this is most likely to happen at the beginning of the negotiation in response to open ended questions.

The advantage of starting with open ended questions is apparent in light of the risks of narrow questions. If you first cover all the topics you think are important, turning to the other person and asking, "Can you think of anything else?" may be a futile effort. Changing to open ended questions at the end may not work for two reasons. First, because you have already extensively discussed various topics, the other person may not be motivated to suggest additional topics.

A second and related problem is that questioners "train" people on appropriate response techniques. The questioner who starts out asking yes/no questions subtly tells the person answering that her appropriate role is to provide brief, concise answers. When later asked an open ended question, the person answering, having played this role throughout the exchange, is unlikely to respond openly. On the other hand, a person you have "trained" to respond to open ended questions is more likely to keep providing lots of information throughout the exchange.

Remember also, that the narrower, more specific questions, "Is Polisi looking for work?" or "Why hasn't she found a new job?" are more threatening, and if asked too soon may hurt the rapport that a cooperative negotiator seeks to achieve. Also, on a practical level, if you remember the specific question early in the interview, you likely will remember it at the end of the interview as well, so you lose little by putting the question off, and you gain much by having patience.

A typical open ended question starting a funnel approach might be as follows:

> *LAWYER FOR PARKER & GOULD (P&G): Will you bring me up to date about Ms. Polisi?*
>
> *ANSWER (A): Well, she's not happy.*
>
> *P&G: Why don't you tell me about it?*
>
> *A: I don't see the necessity, you've gotten discovery.*
>
> *P&G: I'd certainly like to find out where she is today, tell me what you think I need to know to get this thing settled.*
>
> *A: It's what we've been talking about all along. Her reputation is damaged, she's lost income, her future earning power has been impaired, she's very angry, and, justifiably she's hurt.*
>
> *P&G: Anything else?*
>
> *A: Yes. She wants Parker & Gould punished.*
>
> *P&G: Good. I'd like to talk to you about each of those. I, of course, have some questions myself for you and Ms. Polisi.*

This person's reaction to the open ended question, "Will you bring me up to date about Ms. Polisi?" is: "She's not happy." The good negotiator, however, will attempt to keep the questioning open ended and try a different, though still open ended question: "Why don't you tell me about it?" In this example, the person opens up and we see the common response of people to open ended questions in that they seem to talk in lists. With a few questions, the lawyer has elicited a "gush" from the person that contains what appear to be the most important topics they will need to discuss.

The lawyer is now in a position to evaluate what the person has told her. Perhaps more importantly in light of the topics mentioned, as well as topics the lawyer brings to the negotiation, the lawyer can begin to systematically explore various topics. The lawyer can now better decide which topics are important to discuss, and how and in what order.

The open ended question or questions help you to identify various topics that are important to explore. You then add other topics, and decide which topics to explore in which order. The good questioner can now choose whether to discuss items mentioned by the other person first, or discuss items on their own agenda, or items that appear important to both. If developing a rapport remains a primary consideration, you may, for example, prefer to provide the other side with the benefit of meeting their needs first. Each topic, in turn, can be seen as its own funnel for inquiry.

Having decided which topics should be discussed, you should next narrow the inquiry by going to that topic and asking narrower, though still quite open ended, questions. In reality, then, our funnel analogy is really more accurately described as funnels within funnels. Each new topic creates the beginning of a new funnel of inquiry.

OPEN ENDED QUESTION

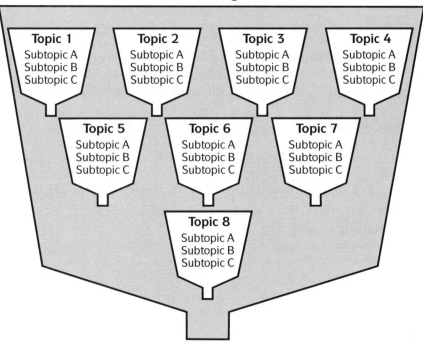

To illustrate this further, assume you are meeting with the lawyer of a company that is interested in purchasing a business owned by your client. The purchasing company is new to you and you feel you need to get a great deal of detailed information before your client is prepared to even consider doing business with them. The meeting might proceed as follows:

> *LAWYER (L): Good. I'd like to talk to you about doing business. I, of course, have some questions about you and your company. Would you tell me about the company?*
>
> *A: Well we are just expanding into this state. We've seen steady growth over the past few years and find ourselves well positioned to expand.*
>
> *L: Tell me more.*
>
> *A: We're family owned. Mr. Duffy's father started the company back in 1950. Duffy senior died about ten years ago and the son took over.*
>
> *L: What else?*
>
> *A: I'm not sure what you mean?*
>
> *L: Tell me some more about the company.*

Note here that the lawyer is trying to keep the questions open ended as long as feasible. At some point the person questioned may question the approach and a narrowing of the questions might have to occur.

> *A: Not much else to say.*
>
> *L: Tell me about its size, level of sales, that type of thing.*
>
> *A: As I said, we're growing. We sell to about 50 percent of the hospitals in the tri-state area. Mostly private hospitals.*

Once the person no longer "gushes," you might narrow the questions by raising additional topics in question form:

> *L: What type of products?*

> *L: Service support?*

> *L: How about inventory?*

> *L: Tell me about yourself.*

These questions are really just topics the lawyer feels are important, but were not raised by the potential purchaser's lawyer in the "gush." Again, however, you should try to keep it as open ended as possible. If your goal is to acquire as much information as possible, the next step is to pick one of these topics and ask about it in an open ended way.

> *L: Awhile back you mentioned you sell to about 50 percent of the hospitals in the tri-state area, tell me more about that.*

Here the lawyer has picked a topic and has begun discussion with a good open ended question that should maximize information. Additional topics should present themselves and the lawyer can choose which are most important to follow up, seeking more and more specific information, or which can be set aside for later discussion. Indeed, the lawyer may choose to address an entirely new topic, feeling that a more general overview is needed and later return to this topic to "complete the funnel."

Completing the systematic exploration of this topic, or any other topic, will require progressively narrower questions. Continuing our example, the series of questions that might follow could look as follows:

"You've mentioned inventory, tell me about your suppliers."

    "Who are they?"

        "Tell me about your relationship with them."

        "Tell me about the financial arrangements."

    "What are the regular trade terms offered to the company?

        "Are there any special terms involved?"

        "Are discounts taken?"

        "Are payments prompt?"

        "Are any items in dispute?"

        "Are contracts or franchises involved?"

        "Tell me about those."

        "When does it (the contract or franchise) expire?"

Having fully explored the topic, or again choosing to hold off on this level of detail at this time, you can choose a new topic and move through the funnel:

    "You mentioned the manufacturing and retail sides, why don't you tell me something about the company's plant and equipment?"

Following the response, necessary follow-up questions (in order of progressing narrowness) may include:

    "Are the facilities owned or leased?"

        "Who owns the leases?"

        "What are the lease terms?

        "Any options?"

        "Where is the facility located?

        "Single purpose or multi-use?"

"Tell me about its operating capacity."

"Is the capacity sufficient for future needs?"

"Anything else you can tell me about the facility?"

Having thus gone through the information in considerable detail, the next stage is to view the information gathered and seek precise details that may not have been mentioned. At this stage, various pre-printed forms are particularly valuable. Also, direct questions, such as costs or discounts which are perhaps too threatening at the beginning of the negotiation, are least likely to adversely affect the interview.

Using the techniques discussed here during a negotiation raise a number of complicating factors. Most obviously, the person on the other side may not be as cooperative as you would like. You might ask the perfect open ended question and he may give you short answers. Also, your attempt to get the "gush" may get you only one topic before you are asked to answer a question. The fact that both sides are seeking information is, of course, why we call it information bargaining. What you must keep in mind, however, is that although the gush may take multiple questions and trickle out in what is difficult to see as a gush, you should make every attempt to keep the inquiry as open ended as possible until you are comfortable that all the important topics are on the table. Spending time eliciting the "gush," even when it comes out in a trickle and requires multiple questions, interrupted by your having to answer the other side's questions, is nonetheless critical.

One of the other main difficulties with open ended questions is that they can be time consuming and in the real world you may not have the luxury of a complete funnel approach. Your initial open ended questions, however, remain critical. The "gush" sets up the solution to the problem that it takes too much time. Where time is limited, the "gush" is critical since it provides you with the list of topics which allow you to decide which important topics on which to spend your limited time.

PROBLEM 6.5

Take the example on pages 68-71 relating to the acquisition of a new business deal with a series of related, though separate topics (e.g., management, inventory, etc.). Quite often, the circumstances surrounding your negotiation involve some prior transaction or occurrence. Rather than having a series of topics that you need to explore, there is a chronological event that must be explored. For example, your client may be having difficulty getting a subcontractor to comply with a contractual obligation or the contractor may be trying to renegotiate the completion of the contractual obligation.

What is the equivalent to the funnel approach when dealing with a chronological problem?

An open ended question that might be appropriate for a chronologically based negotiation is illustrated by the following example:

LAWYER (L): I understand you are having some recent difficulties. Why don't you start at the beginning and take me step by step through the problem?

ANSWER: I'm not sure what you mean.

L: Well, why don't you start at the point when you started the project and take me step by step through what happened?

During this stage, if you want the person to proceed with a chronology, the next appropriate question may simply be, "Then what happened?" Each event mentioned is the equivalent of the funnel within the funnel. You can begin exploring individual parts of the chronology with such questions as, "You mentioned that on September 5, you talked to the bank. Will you tell me about that?"

Many lawyers have gone to negotiations to resolve litigation that has been going on for years, with massive discovery, and asked only specific questions, only to find out later that the other party had undergone financial setbacks and was on the brink of bankruptcy. Never assume that facts have not changed. A good open ended question such as, "Bring me up to date," may save you embarrassment later.

F. Information You Do Not Want to Reveal

During a negotiation whenever someone is asked a question the person would prefer not answering, the person questioned has three choices: tell the truth, avoid the question, or lie. Regardless of other considerations, whichever you choose to do, do it affirmatively. Few people will debate that it is inappropriate to lie in a negotiation. While there may be short-term benefits, given the importance of information, lying can ruin your reputation, hurt your credibility, and destroy any long-term relationship you hope to have.

Revealing the information may be the best course. If you choose to do that, do not hesitate. Do it affirmatively. If you are going to be honest about telling the truth, you might as well get the full benefit from it. Assume Polisi's lawyer is asked:

> *Parker & Gould (P&G): Does Ms. Polisi intend to continue the practice of law?*
>
> *A: Well, uh . . . she has a number of options.*
>
> *P&G: But are there other specific possibilities that she is looking into?*
>
> *A: Well, she's considering teaching law.*

Here Polisi's lawyer ultimately reveals the information without much struggle, but it appears grudging. The truth comes out, but the lawyer loses credibility because it appears he tried to avoid giving the information. If the information is going to come out, get the benefit of communicating your honesty and forthrightness by stating it affirmatively and then putting the proper spin on the information. For example:

> *P&G: Does Ms. Polisi intend to continue the practice of law?*

73

> *A: Her reputation has been so damaged by your clients that her ability to obtain comparable employment in the practice of law is severely limited. She is therefore considering mitigating the damage by teaching law.*

You may choose to avoid revealing the information short of lying, by blocking or fending off the question. There are standard blocks that are used to fend off questions. Take the question from a prospective employee: "What's your standard salary package for new staff?" One type of block is to leave the questioner with the assumption that the question was answered:

> *We've never had an arrangement quite like this. You can't really say we have a standard package.*

A second type of block is to narrow the focus of the question, in this instance perhaps focusing on the word "standard." The answer might be:

> *We really don't have a standard package since each staff member is treated as an individual. That's the kind of hospital we pride ourselves on being. Now, I guess what I'd like to hear from you is . . . .*

A third type of block is to restate the question to your liking:

> *You mean is there a salary package that we always provide no matter who the staff member is and what the relationship is like? We don't have one. Now, I guess what I'd like to hear from you is . . . .*

A fourth block is to destroy the desire for follow-up questions:

> *You mean is there a package we always establish no matter who the staff member is and what the relationship is like? Of course, not. For example, let's take a person with 10 years experience with a major metropolitan hospital, already living in the area, with the ability to start immediately. That person is quite different from the person with limited experience, and the need to provide strong supervision and advanced training. Now, I guess what I'd like to hear from you is . . . .*

A final common block is simply to answer the question that was asked. Too often the question is imprecise, not really asking for the information intended. Nevertheless, the person being questioned hears the question, realizes the intent behind it, and usually answers what was intended, rather than what was actually asked. In our example, the person asked what was the standard package. They probably intended to ask something like, "Given what you already know about me and my experience, what are you prepared to offer me in terms of a specific package?" That is a tough question to avoid. What was actually asked, however, was what is the standard package? An effective block to this imprecise question may be simply to answer the question asked, not the question that was intended to be asked: "We don't have a standard one."

To be effective, the block must be stated affirmatively and be followed with a question of your own so as to shift the initiative from the questioner and avoid follow-up questions.

The real risk of blocks is that if it is perceived by the questioner as a block, you have effectively communicated that you are hiding harmful information. While the questioner may not have the specific information, the person will realize that you would have revealed it if it helped you. Added to this, the questioner may begin to question your credibility. Use blocks carefully.

As with all aspects of negotiation, you must view the use of blocks not only from your perspective, but also from the perspective of the other person. In other words, whether or not you use blocks, the other person might, and you should be aware of them. After asking a question you must train yourself to listen not only for the substance of the answer, but also to determine whether or not the answer is responsive. If the answer is not responsive, it may be a block.

If we look at the standard types of blocks in the *Polisi* negotiation, you might ask: *"Does Polisi intend to continue to practice law?"* The range of blocks might include:

— *"She does not have any current employment."*

— *"She's keeping her options open to all possibilities."*

— *"You mean has she given up on the idea that she should be employed in a major law firm with the potential for a salary in the high six figures?"*

— *"Any decision Ms. Polisi makes will depend on a number of considerations."*

How you handle people who fail to reveal information varies depending on the circumstances. In certain circumstances, doing nothing is appropriate. Simply remember that their refusal to disclose has its own meaning and use that information as you would any other. For example, any of the blocks just covered clearly indicate the person is uncomfortable making the first offer. This suggests they are unsure what the value of their side should be and you should encourage them to expect a lower value.

In some circumstances you may have made the block easy, and you should rephrase your question specifically. Here, the question might be rephrased, "Is Ms. Polisi looking for work other than the active practice of law?" In certain circumstances where you have a sufficiently strong relationship that will withstand it, the appropriate response to a block might be to confront the person: "Boy, Charlie, I haven't heard such bologna since the Presidential debates. Give me an answer." Where the relationship with the person is no longer important the confrontation may also rise to a personal challenge and the anxiety may result in information: "You didn't really answer the question, let me rephrase it . . . ."

Often variations on the same question can get you information that was previously blocked. For example, "Where has Ms. Polisi applied for work?"

Where the other party uses the "There are too many variables to answer that question," block, your best response is probably to take each variable and ask how it affects the answer.

G. Impediments to Questioning

Do not assume that what appears to be a lack of cooperation by someone with whom you are negotiating is always motivated by an attempt to manipulate you. Questioning in a negotiation will not always proceed smoothly. The other person may be nonresponsive or talk about tangential points. Their need for information may be so strong that it runs directly contrary to your attempt to systematically gather information.

Psychologists have identified a series of reasons why people being questioned do not provide clear, accurate, and organized information.[16] While this book is certainly not a treatise on psychology, it helps you to understand the negotiation dynamic if you know some of the more common inhibitors. Only after identifying what is inhibiting the communication process are you able to identify a solution.

---

16. R. Gorden, *Interviewing: Strategy, Tactics and Techniques* (4th ed. 1987).

1. Ego Threat

Self-esteem is a critical factor in most people's psychological make-up. People will often avoid providing information which they believe will place them in a negative image in front of others and hurt their ego. For example, a person who has had a series of financial reversals may be unwilling to provide accurate information for fear that the person will view her as incompetent or foolish.

2. Result Threat

People refuse to give information because they fear it will hurt their attempt to get the result they want. Take, for example, a merger and acquisition negotiation. Business reversals may pose a personal threat, because the fear that the acquiring business in a merger and acquisition will refuse favorable terms as a result of the information.

3. Role Expectation

Society puts individuals into certain roles and others interact with a certain expectation that they will act according to these roles. In a legal negotiation this is most apparent in how the respective lawyers view their roles. The lawyer who believes, or has a client that believes, that lawyers are supposed to be tough, aggressive negotiators, may simply not realize that an alternative exists. The problem goes beyond mere intimidation. If one lawyer views negotiation as a debate over positions, he may be unwilling to give the opposing counsel a correct statement of underlying needs because he expects the opponent to use it against him. Indeed, if you perceive your role as a cooperative problem solver, this misperception can sometimes lead to deadlock, because your attempts to get opposing counsel to open up and talk freely may be met with one- or two-word answers.

Perceived inequality of status can likewise affect your negotiations. If you are negotiating with an older lawyer, you may have to fight the reluctance to defer to the person merely because of status. Similarly, you must not let the person's status intimidate you so you do not ask the questions you need to ask or allow the other lawyer to avoid answering the questions you have asked.

4. Perceived Irrelevancy

If one of our goals is to obtain accurate, relevant, and reliable information, problems can result from the other person having a different view of what is relevant information. A person may simply not mention information because they think it is irrelevant. Further, if you seek what the person perceives as irrelevant information, they may react negatively, hurting rapport and inhibiting your attempts to acquire information.

5. Greater Need

The other person's goals for the negotiation often are such that there is little that can be done to simultaneously meet both your goals and theirs. Imagine a situation where you are talking to a lawyer for the company your client would like to acquire. You may be asking for a great deal of specific information that you can then use to justify a specific proposal, yet in what is clearly intended to be a cooperative, problem-solving negotiation, your opponent avoids answering and talking about what the name of the merged company will be. It may be that this lawyer's client has a need that is greater than the money part of the deal, such as a desire to have his name memorialized.

In *Polisi*, if Parker & Gould are trying to pin down the financial needs of Ms. Polisi, and her attorney keeps talking about vindication, it is a pretty clear indication that Polisi has a higher need. Two things, therefore follow. First, if you are to avoid deadlock, you may have to temporarily give up what you are trying to do to allow you to address this greater need. Second, if you recognize the problem as the opponent having a greater need, you may take advantage of this, especially if your opponent's need is unimportant to you. For example, if Ms. Polisi has a greater need for vindication than money, this indicates she might settle for less money in exchange for a public apology. If it turns out that the apology is not an issue for your client, you can trade your meaningless bargaining chip (an apology) for a blue chip (less money).

6. Forgetting

Human beings forget. Related to forgetting, the person being questioned may be confused or have incomplete memory. Memory is made up of several factors, including not only the original perception at the time, but that perception modified over time by external factors. For example, a lawyer's relationship with a client may be influenced not simply by personal contacts, but by statements of other people who have dealt with the lawyer in the past.

7. Time and Money

Time is a significant factor in most business relationships. A busy person may give less information in order to avoid the added cost of a longer negotiation. Time spent with you is time the person may feel is more profitably spent elsewhere. Trying to negotiate a small claim, for example, may be complicated by the fact that opposing counsel believes she is too busy to discuss such mundane issues as your "little accident." Your task will be to recognize this as a problem and conduct the discussions in a way to minimize this attitude affect.

H. Techniques to Motivate

You can deal with problems inhibiting information gathering in several ways. While none of these are foolproof, they do provide a range of techniques which can be used to encourage the other side to provide information.

1. Education

One of the most effective, and perhaps least used, techniques to get a person to provide information is to educate the person. Quite often, problems which inhibit the questioning result from the person not having a systematic view of the process and not knowing that anything is wrong. By educating the person, you can often reap immediate rewards.

The person giving short answers to open ended questions, or the person who jumps from one topic to the next, might benefit from a simple explanation as to the process you would like to follow:

> *I realize we have a limited amount of time to spend today so I thought we might proceed as follows. I've found that I can most efficiently use your time if I start off with some general questions and have you tell me as much about each topic as you can. I can then go back and ask you for any additional specific information I need. Then we can answer any questions you may have.*

2. Cost-Benefit Analysis

Education will often also help with problems such as loan or ego threat by providing a cost-benefit analysis. For example:

It must be difficult talking about these business reversals. As difficult as it is we need this information. In fact, having it is less harmful than not having it, because we can't resolve this outstanding problem without some very specific information.

3. Empathetic Understanding, Recognition, and Catharsis

Sometimes people come to a negotiation with psychological needs requiring empathy, sympathy, catharsis, or recognition. Often the best technique to get beyond these needs is to provide the empathetic/ sympathetic ear, or the chance for the person to have the catharsis. For example, providing Margaret Polisi a forum to vent past grievances may be extremely helpful to your position if you represent Parker & Gould. By sitting back and listening you may be able to convince her that things have changed. Further, you can provide recognition by statements such as, "This is important information," or "You're providing me with a good background here."

4. Active Listening

Active and passive listening techniques will both foster the giving of information by the person and help maintain an appropriate rapport. Listening techniques range along a continuum from neutral or passive to directive or active. Passive or neutral responses to a person's statement convey little information to the person and are designed to simply indicate that the lawyer is still listening and the person should continue talking. Active or directive responses communicate information, or the lawyer's interpretation of the person's response and, therefore, may direct the person toward new topics or indicate to the person that they need to clarify information already provided. The following are common listening techniques you may find helpful.

• Silence

Silence can be one of the most effective neutral probes for information. People are socialized to abhor silence. We turn on radios without really listening to them; we hum; we have music in elevators. Given silence, most people will seek to fill it with noise. This is as true in the interview as it is in life in general. If you do not speak, chances are that the other person will. Simply waiting as little as a second after the person drops her voice indicating she has finished may be enough to encourage her to continue. This technique is particularly helpful following an open ended question.

- **"Mm-hm"**

Statements such as "Mm-hm," "yes," or "I see," following a comment by the person are neutral probes and communicate that you are listening intently to what is being said. When followed by silence, the statements encourage the listener to keep talking.

- **Restatement**

A slightly more directive listening technique is restating what the person says. Restatement shows the person that you are listening; in fact, listening so intently you are able to repeat the person's exact words. For example:

> *L1: So after the last staff meeting they decided to seriously discuss this attempt to control emergency room activity.*

> *L2: The decision to seriously discuss the attempt to control emergency room activity came after the last staff meeting?*

Restatement is more directive than "Mm-hm" because it may communicate greater interest on the part of the lawyer and, therefore, indicate to the person that you need more information on this topic.

- **Clarification**

Asking for a clarification is more directive than restatement. For example:

> *L1: So after the last staff meeting we decided to seriously discuss this attempt to control the emergency room.*

> *L2: The decision came after the staff meeting. I'm not sure I understand. Was there a connection between the meeting and the decision to change procedure?*

- **Reflection**

Reflection can also help. With reflection, you add an interpretation to the person's statement. Because the interpretation contains information about your perceptions, the statement may be quite directive.

> *L1: So after the last staff meeting we decided to seriously discuss this attempt to control the emergency room.*

> *L2: The decision came after the staff apparently expressed concern over the current condition of the emergency room.*

Not only facts, but feelings can be reflected:

> *L1: So after the last staff meeting we decided to seriously discuss this attempt to control the emergency room.*

> *L2: It sounds like there is some anger about the control.*

I. Nonverbal Communication

In addition to verbal communication you should be as aware of nonverbal communication in a negotiation as you are in an interview.[17] Nonverbal information is often more valuable, since it is often not intended to be communicated and therefore has a higher reliability. Indeed, professional negotiators refer to such unintentional communication (whether verbal or nonverbal) as "leakage."

A complete review of nonverbal communication is beyond the scope of this work. A brief review, however, should emphasize its importance. Nonverbal communication can be divided into four types: chronemics; kinesics; proxemics; and paralinguistics. With regard to each of these, experts have drawn various conclusions, but four generalities particularly apply in legal negotiation and deserve special mention.

First, many experts believe that the effectiveness and usefulness of words tend to be overestimated. Some experts estimate that as much as 60 percent of all important messages are passed nonverbally. An awareness of nonverbal communication is therefore critical for interpersonal communication. Second, not only is a great deal of information passed nonverbally, certain types of gestural language cannot be communicated by words.

A third important point is that some nonverbal information is a physiological response to stress and therefore may be a more accurate indication of information. Blushing, for example, may be a more accurate indication of embarrassment than any words said. Finally, many psychologists believe that there is always what they refer to as message redundancy. In other words, people communicate the same information in multiple ways. A person who is uncomfortable in a particular situation may both wrap his arms around himself and blush. Given that nonverbal communication is subject to interpretation (a person wrapping their arms around themselves may simply be cold),

---

17. There is extensive literature on nonverbal communication. Among the more helpful books are D. Druckman, R. Rozelle, and J. Baxter, *Nonverbal Communication: Survey, Theory and Research* (1982) and A. Mehrabian, *Nonverbal Communication* (1972).

message redundancy allows us to search for a confirming interpretation of a message we think we are receiving nonverbally.

1. Leakage

Almost anything the other side does may leak information. For example, when the other party is coming in from out of town and has arrived the night before, and shows up at your office with a suit bag, "leaks" information that she has checked out of the hotel. This gives you information that as the negotiations take longer and longer, the other side may need to quickly resolve the negotiation or change their travel plans. The additional bother may not make a critical difference, but it may put additional pressure on the other side.

Like any information, you can actively seek leakage. Take our previous example, where the lawyer has to sell a large asset. During the ice breaking stage, the lawyer may bring up the question of whether an out-of-town buyer needs hotel accommodations in order to see if the buyer will "leak" whether they have plans to stay overnight. The lawyer may then determine the time frame with which they have to work.

Two types of leakage merit special mention because of their reoccurrence in negotiation after negotiation. First, there is the leakage resulting from waffle words. These are words that communicate a lack of a firm position. How many times have you or the person you are negotiating with said something like, "We are looking for something between 10 and 15?" You usually cannot ask for a range in a negotiation. The lawyer hearing this range should assume that either 10 or 15 is acceptable, depending on which is more favorable to the lawyer. The only time you should speak of ranges is when you attach conditions to explain the range, such as, "We want 10 to 15 depending on whether . . . ." Also, using the term "looking for" leaks the person will take less. If, for example, 10 were the person's real bottom line, it is likely they would have been more affirmative and emphatic saying, "We want 10."

A concession pattern can also leak information. As you approach your bottom line or commitment point, concessions tend to get smaller and smaller and faster and faster. If you listen and keep track of the size and speed of concessions, you may get a sense of whether the latest concession is truly the bottom line.

2. Chronemics

Chronemics, or the use of time to communicate, can take many forms. A lawyer can communicate a great deal about the importance of the negotiation based on their use of time. If they squeeze the negotiation in between two other meetings they obviously do not highly value the negotiation. Also, a lawyer who is chronically late communicates information concerning his perception of the relationship.

3. Kinesics

Kinesics is the use of the body to communicate. Interestingly enough, researchers indicate that most people focus on the face of the other person in an interview. They also believe the face reveals the most accurate information. Research also indicates, however, that a listener tends to watch the other speaker's eyes more closely than a speaker watches the listener's. The lesson from the research seems clear. We should continue to be aware of the face as a primary source of information, but be aware that some non-verbal information may be missed by failure to watch the entire body.

Examples of kinesics are familiar to most people. With respect to body posture, slouching may connote lack of concern or defeat. Feet movements or tapping or swaying of legs and feet may show nervousness. Hand movements, such as placing the hand over the mouth when talking, may show the speaker is unsure about the statement being made. Facial expressions can communicate a wide range of information including disgust, anger, sadness, and joy. Eye movements are also significant, such as rolling or darting eyes showing disbelief or anxiety.

4. Proxemics

Proxemics is using the environment to communicate. We have already discussed a major environmental control in the negotiation when we discussed where the negotiation should take place, including arranging furniture and people's ability to control intrusions into their space.

Psychologists also tell us that objects such as flower vases and abstract sculpture in a negotiation setting tend to facilitate informality and cooperative behavior. Books in a negotiation setting tend to inhibit informality and cooperative behavior. Round tables increase informality and feelings of closeness.

Proxemics is at play in other contexts as well. As with all non-verbal communication, proxemics is subject to interpretation and the interviewer needs to seek confirmation of the information. For example, when you are greeted at the door (or when you greet someone) do they move toward you indicating they are pushy, aggressive, assertive, or anxious to get to know you? Or do they (or you) step back, indicating they are welcoming, passive, or easily manipulated?

Furniture placement within a room can either facilitate or inhibit communication. As a general rule, locating large objects between people decreases communication. If you wish to develop a cooperative, caring relationship, it makes sense not to interview the person from behind a large desk. Sitting side by side is perhaps best. On the other hand, in many cultures being physically close can inhibit communication. As with most areas in dealing with interpersonal skills, flexibility is an advantage. A furniture arrangement that lets you choose how close to sit can facilitate communication. In addition, the type of furniture can impact the flow of communication. Chairs with wheels can help as can chair and loveseat arrangements. With a chair and loveseat arrangement, you can sit in the chair and the person can adjust proximity by choosing where to sit on the loveseat.

5. Paralinguistics

Paralinguistics is the use of the voice itself to communicate meaning. Voice quality, for example, whether it is tense or breathy, will communicate very different messages. The pitch, pace, tone, and volume of the voice all work together to communicate different messages. A deliberative mood, for example, can be communicated by a slower rate of speech. A high pitch, fast pace, or high volume may communicate lack of time or patience.

Placing the stress on a different word in the same sentence can also greatly affect its meaning. The simple sentence "I did not call Alice a crook" takes on a variety of meanings based on which word is emphasized. The variety is almost limitless, but can range anywhere from having said nothing negative about anyone, to having called someone other than Alice a crook, to having called Alice a name, but not the name "crook."

Not all non-verbal communication fits nicely into only one of these categories. Perhaps one of the most common examples of proxemics and kinesics combined in an interview is the speaker's moving toward or away from someone during the interview. This changing of the environment by leaning the body can communicate a great deal about the interest or lack of interest the person has. Also, it can indicate the degree of comfort the person feels toward you. Finally, it is not important what label we apply to the behavior as long as we are aware of what messages we are sending and what messages the person has sent.

As you can see from the above, information bargaining is an important phase of any negotiation. The saying "knowledge is power" certainly applies to the negotiation setting. Your quest for information about the other side will pervade much of the process, and you should never let an opportunity to add to your information about their position slip by. Next, we will address the actual give and take of a negotiation—the exchange.

Chapter 7

EXCHANGE

A. The Offer

Eventually, one of the negotiators will suggest a solution to what is being negotiated. Whether we call the solution an offer, a demand, or a proposal, an effective solution has a number of common elements. If you ask yourself what you are trying to accomplish with your proposal, it becomes clear that on a broad level there are two goals. First, you want the proposal to be perceived as fair, just, and equitable, and one that meets everyone's needs to the extent possible. Common sense tells you that if the parties do not believe the proposal meets these criteria, it is unlikely to be accepted.

However, another equally important goal exists. You must also persuade the other side that you have nothing else to offer. Whether phrased in the harsh language of a competitive adversarial that "The offer is fair and you won't get a dime more!" or in the terms of a problem solver that "It's fair and I can't think of a better solution," you will not reach an agreement if the other side believes that, despite the offer's fairness, more favorable terms are available.

The difficulty with this second goal is that you must persuade the other side that you will offer nothing else, knowing that down the road you may very well give some more. You must make the proposal, therefore, in a manner that is both persuasive and does not undercut your credibility when later it turns out that (as an adversarial) you make a concession or (as a problem solver) reformulate your proposed solution.

B. Justification and Persuasion

1. Reasons for Everything

Providing reasons for your position is an essential element of any attempt to negotiate systematically. To give your proposal credibility you must provide reasons to justify it as fair, just, and equitable, as well as reasons why you will not give more. An unsupported proposal does little to persuade the other side of anything other than that you picked a particular number or other solution out of the air. If you will pick one number out of the air why won't you pick another number more favorable to the other side? Reasons help you persuade the other side that the proposal is fair, just, and equitable and that you are not prepared to offer more.

2. Objective Criteria Arguably Beyond Your Control

Perhaps the most important component to persuasion in negotiation is the use of objective criteria that are arguably beyond your control. Objective criteria are more persuasive than subjective. When the defense lawyer is negotiating with plaintiff's counsel and says, "We won't pay more than $70,000 because it is fair," the statement is unpersuasive. Fair to whom, based on what criteria? Wouldn't $75,000 be fairer? Saying "$75,000 is all I can offer because of restrictions by the insurance company," is marginally more persuasive. A semi-objective reason—they won't let me do it—supports this statement, but the reason is not beyond the control of the lawyer's client.

Saying "$75,000 is our offer—it makes sense given that's what we settled a similar claim for last week," is much more persuasive. Here, the statement is supported by an objective indicator of the "market" price, which is arguably beyond defense counsel's control because it is either set by the nebulous concept of "the market" or by other plaintiffs' attorneys.

Even proposals involving something less quantifiable than money, such as work schedules, are more persuasive when they are objective.

> *Labor Lawyer: The schedule's simply not fair. Look at the schedules over the past three months. During that time union employees have consistently been denied overtime on weekends. Here, let me show you . . . .*

Anybody with an adjustable rate mortgage, home equity line, or credit card has experienced discomfort over the bank's ability to control interest rates. This discomfort is in part related to this issue of objective criteria. Customers frequently reject pricing on such adjustable rate loans if based on prime plus some percentage point. One possible reason for this rejection is that, while prime is objective, the customer may not perceive it as beyond the bank's control. The offer does not sound fair, just, and equitable, because there may be an underlying fear that the bank will arbitrarily increase prime. Basing the rate on something like the cost of funds to the bank (such as United States Treasury Bills), however, may sound more persuasive because, whether correct or not, customers perceive it as less subject to the bank's control. The fact that the bank's prime is driven by cost of funds, and that all pricing whether based on prime or cost of funds is ultimately controlled by market forces, is irrelevant to this customer. A rate based on the cost of funds is more attractive because it appears beyond the control of the bank.

Often the most difficult part of making a persuasive statement is identifying the objective criteria that can be used to justify a subjective issue. Imagine the lawyer engaged in setting up a health maintenance organization or managed care facility. The lawyer must negotiate with various private physician groups to get them to join the new organization. The lawyer might have problems persuading a potential group practice that the proposed business relationship actually will provide a better level of service for the group's patients. Lawyers representing the promoters of the new business entity must identify objective measures of patient satisfaction and quality of service to support their proposal. Statistics concerning patient turnover, new business, or the like might be persuasive in this example.

In a merger or acquisition negotiation, there might be an issue of distrust between two previously competing businesses. Identifying a way to quantify trust can be quite challenging, but pointing to specific trust-building measures in other acquisitions may be helpful. For example, the acquiring company's showing that it has a good record for employee retention following an acquisition can be objective and persuasive. Also, making a specific commitment public by way of a press release may make the commitment seem beyond the control of the negotiator and therefore more permanent and consequently more persuasive.

The connection between effective client counseling and the ability to develop objective criteria should be apparent. Having the client identify what they would like to accomplish is clearly an essential step. Getting the client to help you identify the potential rationales for why that result is appropriate is equally important.

PROBLEM 7.1

In *Polisi v. Parker & Gould*, Ms. Polisi has indicated that her primary goal is to get as much money from Parker & Gould as possible. **What objective criteria, arguably beyond your control, can be used to justify a particular high settlement?**

Assume instead that Ms. Polisi has indicated that money is not nearly as important as getting a new job, having sufficient cash flow during the job search and get an apology. **What objective criteria, arguably beyond your control can be used to justify a particular high settlement?**

Identifying objective criteria, of course, depends on the particular facts associated with a negotiation. However, the criteria must be something valued by the person with whom you are negotiating. For example, in the above problem, a reasonably safe working premise (that we will of course check out during information bargaining) would be that Parker & Gould value money and reputation. To maximize the amount of money Ms. Polisi can demand, a number of criteria suggest themselves. Clearly jury verdict research is an important criteria. Past jury verdicts are both objective and arguably beyond the control of the parties, and the more similar the case, the more persuasive the analogy. A typical persuasive statement based on jury verdicts might go:

Our client has authorized me to accept $730,000 to settle this case. Let me explain how we have arrived at this figure. We have done extensive research on verdicts in these types of cases. Independent of our own research we have consulted with Jury Verdict Research, Inc. I have its report here, as well as a listing of similar cases involving sexual harassment and defamation against professional women. You will see that the verdicts range between 375,000 and 1.3 million dollars. Given the public nature of this dispute and the fact that Ms. Polisi is in the higher income bracket among the plaintiffs in these cases (the 1.3 million was a physician, we have a $950,000 verdict for a lawyer), at least a $950,000 verdict is likely. We recognize, of course, that between trial and appeals we are looking at four years to recover that amount. So we are willing to reduce it to its present value. Our accountant tells us that the present value of $950,000 in four years is $775,000. We estimate that we will also save $45,000 in litigation expenses. Subtract that and you get $730,000.

Jury verdicts are not the only objective criteria. Experts in an appropriate field often provide value data upon which to base offers and persuasive statements. Indeed, choosing different criteria can result in vastly different offers. Read the following material prepared by Gerald Stoller, Ph.D.,[18] as part of Bocchino and Sonenshein, *Polisi v. Clark and Parker & Gould: Advanced Case File* (NITA, 1994). The expert has provided information valuable not only for the jury but for the negotiation.

---

18. The Center for Forensic Economic Studies, Suite 12, 1608 Walnut Street Philadelphia, PA 19103, (215) 546-5600.

REPORT OF ECONOMIC LOSS

POLISI v. CLARK AND PARKER & GOULD

PREPARED FOR COUNSEL FOR THE PLAINTIFF

by GERALD MORRIS, Ph.D.

YR-0

This report was prepared for the *Polisi* file by Gerald Stoller, Ph.D. of The Center For Economic Studies, Suite 1200, 1608 Walnut Street, Philadelphia, PA 19103, (215) 546-5600.

Report of Economic Loss
Polisi v. Clark and Parker & Gould
YR-0

INTRODUCTION

This report assesses the economic loss suffered by Margaret Polisi as a result of the alleged gender discrimination and defamation of character, which occurred while she was an employee of the Defendant law firm, Parker & Gould (P & G), and under the supervision of Defendant Clark. The economic loss consists of lost earnings. In reaching these conclusions we have relied on all of the pleadings and other discovery in this case, as well as those other sources that are specifically mentioned in this report.

BACKGROUND

After receiving a bachelor's degree in political science from Nita University in YR-19, Ms. Polisi began her employment in YR-17 as a paralegal at P & G. In YR-13 she entered a four year law degree program in the evening division at the University of Nita School of Law. Ms. Polisi continued to work for the Defendant law firm as a law clerk during her period of attendance at the law school, and during this time received very good performance reviews from her supervisors. Ms. Polisi graduated first in her class from law school in YR-9 and was offered and accepted a position as an associate with P & G. She was assigned to the litigation section of the firm and worked in that section from September of YR-9 through December of YR-2. In June of YR-2, Ms. Polisi was considered for a partnership with the firm, but despite excellent work reviews by her supervisors, was not accepted. She was terminated by the firm, effective December 31, YR-2.

After undergoing a period of psychological trauma brought on by a hostile work environment, she was able to accept a part-time teaching position at the University of Nita School of Law. Eventually she was offered a tenure-line appointment to the law school

94

which commenced in September of YR-1. Ms. Polisi in currently 41 years old and employed as an Associate Professor of Law at the University of Nita.

ASSUMPTIONS

The following assumptions were made in estimating the economic loss to Ms. Polisi:

1. Retirement Age

In our analysis we have assumed that Ms. Polisi will work until the age of 65.

2. Potential Earnings Absent Discrimination and Defamation

At counsel's request, we have provided in our analysis two estimates of the economic loss to Ms. Polisi. We have assessed Ms. Polisi's alleged economic loss as a result of: a) gender discrimination; and b) defamation of character.

Discrimination

We have assumed that the economic loss to Ms. Polisi is a direct result of the alleged gender discrimination she incurred as an employee at P & G. We have valued her potential earnings absent the discrimination as Ms. Polisi's potential earnings as a partner at P & G. According to the information received from P & G, their partners have the following earning pattern:

Years as Partner	Average Earnings (YR-0 dollars)
1	$100,000
3	$135,000
5	$200,000
7	$250,000
10	$300,000
20	$325,000

We have assumed that Ms. Polisi would have become a partner at P & G in June, YR-2, and would have had earnings following the pattern outlined above. We have valued earnings from June of YR-2 to Ms. Polisi's age 65.

95

Defamation

We have assumed that Ms. Polisi did not suffer from
gender discrimination, but that her character was
defamed thereby resulting in an economic loss. Absent
the defamation, Ms. Polisi may have secured alternative
employment at another law firm. However, given the
alleged defamation, she was unable to secure alternative
employment at another law firm. Her potential earnings
absent the defamation are equal to earnings at an
alternative law firm. We have assumed that she would
have secured such employment as of January 1, YR-1. We
have further assumed that she would have remained an
associate until January 1, YR+2 at the alternative firm
and then would have been promoted to partner. Our
assumption is that her earnings would have followed the
pattern set out below:

Year	Position	Average Earnings (YR-0 dollars)
YR-1	Associate	$ 75,000
YR-0	Associate	$ 80,000
YR+1	Associate	$ 90,000
YR+2	Partner	$100,000
YR+4	Partner	$115,000
YR+6	Partner	$125,000
YR+8	Partner	$150,000
YR+11	Partner	$175,000
YR+21	Partner	$200,000

This earnings pattern has been derived reviewing a
national survey of lawyer earning published in the *Nita
Bar Journal* in YR-1. In this estimate we have assumed
that Ms. Polisi's earnings would have been equal to the
median earnings for all partners. This is in contrast
to potential earnings at P & G, a top level law firm
with the earnings to match.

3. Future Growth of Earnings

Earnings growth after YR-1 was estimated to be 6.61%
per year. This rate represents the average annual rate
of change in the Compensation Per Hour Index from YR-21

to YR-1 (*Economic Report of the President*, January YR-0; *Economic Indicators*, March, YR-0.

4. Discount Rate

We have discounted future earnings to their present value. Based on a review of information in this matter and currently prevailing interest rates, we have used a nominal rate of 5%.

5. Earnings in Mitigation

In the Spring of YR-1, Ms. Polisi became an adjunct professor at the University of Nita School of Law. She became a member of the tenure- line faculty in September of YR-1. Her starting salary was $58,000 per year.

We have assumed that Ms. Polisi will remain in the teaching profession and that by YR+7 she will be promoted to a full professor position with a salary of $85,000 per year. This $85,000 figure is based upon data from the University of Nita School of Law as to the average annual salaries of full professors.

It should be noted that we have valued earnings starting in June of YR-2. For earnings from June 1 to December 31, YR-2 we have used Ms. Polisi's salary as an associate at P & G, $73,120.

6. Future Growth and Discounting of Earnings

We have utilized the same future growth and discounting methodologies as described earlier.

TABLES

Table 1 shows earnings as a partner at P & G to age 65.

Table 2 shows earnings as an associate/partner at an alternative law firm to age 65.

Table 3 shows earnings as a law professor to age 65.

SUMMARY

As outlined in the Summary Table, the total economic loss to Ms. Polisi ranges from $2,297,491 to $6,133,374.

SUMMARY TABLE
MARGARET POLISI

DISCRIMINATION

Earnings Absent the Incident	$8,588,104
Less:	
Earnings Given the Incident	$2,254,730

Total Economic Loss	$6,333,374

DEFAMATION

Earnings Absent the Incident	$4,742,221
Less:	
Earnings Given the Incident	$2,454,730

Total Economic Loss	$2,287,491

TABLE 1

EARNINGS ABSENT THE INCIDENT AS A PARTNER AT P & G

PAST TOTAL EARNINGS (YR-2 - YR-0)	$ 310,000
FUTURE TOTAL EARNINGS (YR+1 - YR+24)	$8,277,609
TOTAL EARNINGS	$8,587,609

TABLE 2

**EARNINGS ABSENT THE INCIDENT
AS AN ASSOCIATE/PARTNER
AT ANOTHER FIRM**

PAST TOTAL EARNINGS (YR-1 - YR-0)	$ 155,000
FUTURE TOTAL EARNINGS (YR+1 - YR+24)	$4,597,221
TOTAL EARNINGS	$4,752,221

TABLE 3

**EARNINGS GIVEN THE INCIDENT
AS A LAW SCHOOL PROFESSOR**

PAST TOTAL EARNINGS (YR-2 - YR-0)	$ 162,406
FUTURE TOTAL EARNINGS (YR+1 - YR+24)	$2,292,323
TOTAL EARNINGS	$2,454,729

3. Argumentation

One of the best analyses of what makes arguments persuasive was done by Professor Robert Condlin. A few of the elements of persuasion identified by Professor Condlin and others are helpful to review.[19]

a. Be Detailed

The more detail you provide to support your position, the more persuasive it will usually be. The statement, "The schedule is fair because it is consistent with what is happening at other comparable businesses," is objective and arguably beyond management's control. Compare, however, the statement:

> *Before we made the schedule, I checked around. I checked the other comparable employers. At Metropolitan the average amount of overtime for workers is 40 hours for the last six months. During that same period the average has been 35 hours for City as well as University hospital. Here we see that each union member in this department has averaged 36 hours during the last six months. Here, let me show you our schedule . . . .*

The second statement has the same rationale as the previous example, but it is more persuasive because it contains detailed information about how the schedule was created and compares to others.

Detail often requires proof. For example, when we justified $730,000 based on jury verdict research in the previous scenario, the statement was quite detailed and the lawyer was prepared to provide documentary proof that she had not just pulled the figures out of the air. Providing copies of the economist's report (as well as his curriculum vitae) might be helpful.

b. Multi-dimensional Reasoning

As a general rule, more supporting reasons make your position more persuasive. If you can show that no matter which way you look at a problem the solution always seems to be the same, the solution will more likely be perceived as fair, just and equitable. A simple car negotiation involving the purchase of a used car illustrates the point:

---

19. Condlin, "Cases on Both Sides": Patterns of Argument in Legal Dispute-Negotiation, 44 Md. L. Rev. 65 (1985). See also R. Bastrass & J. Harbaugh, *Interviewing, Counseling, and Negotiation* (1990).

BUYER: I'll give you $15,000 for your car.

SELLER: Too low, the ad says $16,000, and I'm not going any lower.

BUYER: But, wait, look at this. I checked the blue book value on this car. Here, see for yourself. The wholesale price listed is $16,500, the retail price is $17,000. But, you need to, according to the book, subtract $750 for high mileage. That makes the price $15,750. Then you have to figure the tires need to be replaced, that's another $150 apiece so we're at $15,150. Bottom line is I'm also going to have to have the engine looked into and you have said yourself there hasn't been any brake work. That's bound to be needed, so $15,000 is right.

SELLER: I don't know . . . .

BUYER: $15,000 also makes sense from what I see in the market. Look at these other advertisements. Here's the same make and model, a year newer for $17,000. Here's the same make and model, but a year older for $14,500. Also, you are the one who told me the dealer wouldn't give you what you thought the car was worth in trade-in. You'll do better with my $15,000 than the dealer's trade-in value. Don't forget that if you take it today, you can cancel the insurance right away, that will save you a couple of bucks, and you avoid the hassle and expense of trying to find someone else.

Here the persuasive statement points out five reasons why $15,000 is the correct price: 1) blue book value; 2) market price based on other advertisements; 3) can't get a better price at dealer; 4) time savings; and 5) money savings. Individually each of the arguments have a different persuasive force. The blue book argument is objective and beyond the control of the parties. It is also highly detailed. The blue book argument, however, has a major flaw in that the buyer does not explain picking the wholesale price as a starting point; that is not really beyond the control of the party. The other advertisement argument is objective, but lacks detail. The final three arguments are beyond the buyer's control, but lack detail and objectivity. Taken together, however, they are more persuasive than taken alone, and create a more compelling rationale.

The same affect can be used in a number of situations. For example, assume the lawyer's client is seeking to sell the multimillion dollar item:

> BUYER (B): You're the seller. What's the bottom line?
>
> LAWYER (L): Two million dollars.
>
> B: How did you arrive at that figure?
>
> L: It seemed a fair price in light of existing circumstances. We know replacement cost is $2.3. Original cost was $1.75 The price should be somewhere in between.
>
> B: What about depreciation?
>
> L: I look at depreciation this way. This is more like a vintage car than a Chevy. Initially there is going to be some depreciation, but with rising costs its value has got to increase. Its value won't catch up to a new unit, but kept in condition it could well never go below its original cost and may well increase in value as well.
>
> B: But what's magic about $2.0 million?
>
> L: It's not magic. Look at it from my perspective. This unit is an investment. A reasonable return on an investment like this would be 10 percent a year and that's $250,000 for the past two years. Do the math, without compounding, $1.75 million plus $250,000 is $2 million. Two million is also consistent with the recent appraisal we had on the unit.

Here the lawyer has used replacement costs, appreciation based on original cost, return on investment, and an appraisal. Each is objective and arguably beyond the control of the lawyer. For example, she did not create the concept of appreciation, it exists in the real world. Clearly some of the rationales are more beyond the control of the lawyer than others. The lawyer did, after all, pick how much appreciation and probably also selected who was going to be the appraiser. Taken as a whole, however, the arguments are more persuasive than taken individually.

c. Balanced Arguments

Proposals have to be fair, just, and equitable to both sides. Any rationale that merely focuses on one side is inherently less persuasive. No matter how objective, detailed, and multi-dimensional the argument you make, if you focus solely on the needs, interests, and desires of your client, the other person will react with, "What's in it for me? This deal needs to meet my needs as well." The argument requires, therefore, a balanced rationale that shows how it meets both side's needs, interests, and desires.

However, the argument also cannot focus solely on the other side's goals. A persuasive statement that never shows what you get out of the proposal may cause the other person to question your credibility. The negotiation involves meeting both side's goals. If you fail to articulate the rationale by which the proposal meets your needs, the person with whom you are negotiating may think you have hidden something and are afraid to reveal some benefit you seek.

d. Emphatic and Emotional

If you do not believe in your position, why should anyone else? You must communicate conviction by being appropriately emotional and emphatic. While this does not mean tears, it does mean being affirmative and not equivocating. Compare the following statements.

Wrong:

The most we are willing to offer is in the neighborhood of $300,000.

We're looking at $300,000 and the client does not want to make an apology.

Correct:

The client will pay only $300,000, the terms must be confidential, and there certainly won't be an apology.

Wrong:

I don't know, it's unlikely I could get approval for that offer.

Correct:

That offer is unacceptable.

e. Certain Arguments Must Be Subtle

Despite the fact that most arguments are persuasive when they are detailed, some arguments are actually less effective with detail. Take a variation on merger and acquisition negotiation:

L1: You're buying, what's the bottom line?

L2: Six million dollars.

L1: How did you arrive at that figure?

L2: It seemed fair in light of existing circumstances. We know book value is 6.85. Our start-up costs would be $3 million. And we value the goodwill at $1 million. That's $4 million. The price should be somewhere in between.

L1: What about my client's experience?

L2: That's a separate issue. We will agree to continue his employment at $100,000. And besides, let's face it. Your client needs to sell. From what I can tell, you don't have much choice. From what you've told me there's no other purchaser available and he doesn't have the resources to compete.

Put yourself in the position of the client who is to be acquired. How would you feel if you were in the position and this argument were made to you? Would there be a chance that you would react negatively on a basic personal level, and decide, no matter how badly you wanted to sell the business you would not be so blatantly pushed around?

Certain arguments simply cause people to act in a non-rational manner. They force people to take action, as discussed in Chapter 3, not because the action takes them toward their rationally determined goal, but because of some social-psychological reason. Here the threat to the seller's ego by such a direct personal challenge might force the seller to walk out. When it is likely that an argument will precipitate non-rational behavior *and* you are confident the other person will make a detailed argument to themselves, the argument should be subtle. Change the last paragraph in our previous example to:

> *Let me tell you, we appreciate your willingness to talk to us and have no intention of taking advantage of today's tight market conditions.*

You can be assured the other party will fill in the details of that tight market, including the fact that no alternative purchaser exists. In fact, you could probably be even more subtle and not mention the tight market at all. If the seller's need and limitation of options has already been mentioned as part of the information bargaining, you can be confident that the tight market argument will be made in the seller's own mind regardless of what you say or do not say.

4. The Role of Threats

Threats are among the most over used tactics in negotiation. As with the use of subtlety, ask yourself how you feel when threatened? The fact is, threats increase the likelihood that a person will respond non-rationally. And the use of threats decreases the likelihood that the type of relationship necessary for effective problem-solving and long-term trust will develop. In fact, social-psychology research indicates that using threats actually decreases the chance that you will achieve a mutually acceptable result.

While threats are often inappropriately used, research indicates that they can be effective. Whether you choose to use a threat or need to respond to a threat, your first step is to determine what makes a threat effective.

To be effective, a threat must meet a number of elements. First, the threat must be heard. If the threatened party cannot hear the threat, the threat will be ineffective. This suggests that one appropriate response to a threat is simply to ignore it. Pretend you did not hear it, that it simply was not made. Another effective tactic is to call a halt, or recess to the negotiation, if it appears that a threat is likely to occur.

To be effective a threat also must be understood as a threat. For example, a common threat is to let other people in the community know how uncooperative—demanding—unreasonable, or the like, you are. Treating this as a non-threat can be effective.

> *LAWYER FOR POLISI: I don't think the clients of Parker & Gould will be happy when they find out about the behavior of senior partners.*

LAWYER FOR PARKER & GOULD: I think our clients will be pleased to know we don't cave in to unsubstantiated charges. We have a reputation for aggressive litigation, and our clients would expect us to act consistent with that reputation.

An effective threat must also involve an issue that is valued by the person being threatened:

LAWYER FOR POLISI: I don't think the clients of Parker & Gould will be happy when they find out about the behavior of senior partners.

LAWYER FOR PARKER & GOULD: I think Polisi should know from working at the firm that Parker & Gould doesn't care what other firms think. It has a reputation for aggressive behavior that might offend people. The fact that there are these unsupported charges won't make people think any less of the firm.

The threat must also be believed to be effective. Rejecting the possibility that the threat will be carried out may be effective. This may actually simply require ignoring the threat. If you are negotiating with a lawyer who threatens to sue if your client does not comply with some demand, you can usually safely ignore the threat if you know from advance preparation that this particular lawyer has not filed a lawsuit in recent history.

To be effective, a threat must also be prospective:

Lawyer 1: When other staff hear this you will . . . .

Lawyer 2: I already have the reputation of being . . . .

Finally, a threat must be proportionate or totally irrational. If it is neither, ignore it.

A much different approach to dealing with threats used by problem solvers focuses on why people make threats. Social psychologists tell us that people often make threats when they have no other tactic to use. If this is the case, the appropriate response to a threat is to provide the negotiator with an alternative approach to pursue. Take, for example, the situation where you offer a proposal, and the other person responds with, "Well, we're just going to have to sue." An appropriate response might be to get the person to focus on the more principled, systematic approach and invite them to participate:

> *Lawyer: That is one alternative, of course. Before you do that, let me ask you to share with me why you think my position is so unreasonable?*

You might even go so far as to suggest criticism of your detailed persuasive statement.

> *Lawyer: That is one alternative, of course. Before you do that, let me ask you to share with me why you think my position is so unreasonable? For example, how else can we value the loss you allege your client has suffered?*

C. Concessions, Reformulations, and Counter Proposals

The difficult part of making a concession is doing it and maintaining your credibility. If after making a persuasive argument you make a subsequent concession, you run the risk of losing credibility. After all, when you made your previous proposal you said that you are not going to give one more dime and now you are reaching into your pocket for another dime. The risk you run is that the concession will undercut your credibility. After your last offer you said there was no more to give and that was not true. Why should your opponent believe this time that more concessions will not be coming? The task, therefore, is to make concessions while maintaining your credibility, that is, not communicating that your last offer was pulled out of the air. If they believe that the first offer was pulled out of the air, they may believe that the new offer was also pulled out of the air and therefore wait for yet another concession. This is a particularly significant problem if you are already at your bottom line and they do not believe that you are. Deadlock is the likely result.

The principal way to make a concession while maintaining your credibility is to only make a concession that in some way is related to your prior proposal's justification. Usually this means being sure that the other side sees that you are conceding because you have been persuaded that there is something about your original justification that requires the concession.

The problem of "splitting the difference" illustrates the point. Assume our objective, detailed rationale developed previously:

Our client has authorized me to accept $730,000 to settle this case. Let me explain how we have arrived at this figure. We have done extensive research on verdicts in these types of cases. Independent of our own research we have consulted with Jury Verdict Research, Inc. I have their report here, as well as a listing of similar cases involving sexual harassment and defamation against professional women. You will see that the verdicts range between 375,000 and 1.3 million dollars. Given the public nature of this dispute and the fact that Ms. Polisi is in the higher income bracket among the plaintiff's in these cases (the 1.3 million was a physician, we have a $950,000 verdict for a lawyer), at least a $950,000 verdict is likely. We recognize, of course, that between trial and appeals we are looking at four years to recover that amount. So we are willing to reduce it to its present value. Our accountant tells us that the present value of $950,000 in four years is $775,000. We, estimate that we will also save $45,000 in litigation expenses. Subtract that and you get $730,000.

Assume the other lawyer has countered with $500,000 and after a number of hours without movement the other lawyer says, "Why don't we just split the difference, we'll give you $615,000."

If you split this difference, what does it communicate about your original rationale? Logic would indicate that if you are now willing to move $115,000 for no reason other than it is the mid-point between two positions, the original detailed objective rationale was a pretext. You may not care about maintaining credibility at this point. However, if you need to be concerned about this because you, or your client, expects to deal with the other side in the future, you need to find a rationale for the move. For example, you can move from $730,000 to $615,000 and maintain credibility if the move is either explicitly or implicitly tied to one of your original reasons.

Lawyer for Polisi: I have checked around, and the $730,000 makes sense based on an expected verdict of $950,000. You are asking us to essentially discount about 15 percent. Based on what, risk at trial?

Lawyer for Parker & Gould: Yes. Juries are unpredictable.

Lawyer for Polisi: Well, I'll take that back to my client.

Here the lawyer has moved, but in a way that does not say the previous offer was a lie. The lawyer moves in a way that communicates the new figure is rationally based and unlikely to change.

If you follow this approach, you may find yourself in the position of wanting to concede, but being unable to because the person has been unable to think of a way to convince you. You may have to help the other person, as the lawyer for Polisi did in the previous example, by suggesting a reason for the $115,000 concession.

Finally, even if settlement does not come immediately after an offer to split the difference, do not forget that the lawyer who made the suggestion has already indicated that the mid-point is acceptable. The practical result is that you should usually read the offer to split the difference as a unilateral concession of the suggested amount.

This same general approach should be followed by both problem solvers as well as adversarial negotiators. A couple of differences, however, will be noted. First, since problem solvers are trying to develop a joint solution to the problem, they typically do not refer to offers and demands. They prefer to use words and phrases such as proposal, solution, proposed solution, or "an idea to throw out on the table." Second, problem solvers often invite the other side to critically analyze their proposal as a way of generating suggestions for improving it. Third, because the problem solver is seeking a creative solution, they are normally less committed to a specific proposal, that is, they are more willing to reformulate an idea, and have less pride of authorship. Fourth, a problem solver will avoid using terms such as concession and compromise, since the words denote positional bargaining. Rather, problem solvers will "take a suggestion and reformulate a proposal."

D. Typical Exchange Tactics and a Systematic Approach

You will find in today's literature on negotiation a wide variety of negotiating tactics to become an effective negotiator. Some of these tactics we have already discussed in the context of a systematic approach to negotiation. The purpose of this text is to suggest that a systematic, principled approach will be more effective than a series of "tricks of the trade." However, many of these tactics may well fit within the systematic approach presented here as examples of specific phases. Also, thinking about how these tactics fit within the systematic approach often helps to decide how to counter the tactic when it is used against you.

While a complete review of all these suggested tactics is beyond the scope of this work, a review of some of the more common suggestions is offered to support what was said earlier. There are no rules; there are only choices to make. Using any specific tactic makes sense only if it fosters the systematic approach you have chosen and is appropriate in this specific negotiation at this specific time.

1. Anger

Negotiators sometimes resort to feigned anger as a means of trying to convince an opponent that they are serious about their position. They also use it to intimidate. Real anger is the result of frustration or anxiety and is often not consciously intended to do anything.

Real anger can be quite dangerous. Anyone who loses control because of frustration and anxiety runs the risk of communicating more than they wish. The mere act of becoming angry, if real, communicates frustration or anxiety, which itself may be important information to the other side. Also, the substance of any outburst may result in inadvertently revealing information. For example, a lawyer involved in a negotiation over merger of two corporations might at the prospect of deadlock blurt out, "Your arrogance is overwhelming . . . ." Assuming the anger is not feigned, the outburst communicates important information about how the lawyer is being perceived by the lawyer making the outburst. The lawyer subject to the outburst can choose either to foster that anger or, if she believes it is counter-productive, take steps to diffuse the anger. The outburst, for example, may reflect that a deadlock is not over the substance of the negotiation, but is the result of a clash of personalities. The lawyer subject to the outburst, therefore, might choose to try to break the deadlock by diffusing the personality clash rather then trying to make a substantive concession such as offering more money.

If you use feigned anger be careful. The anger may induce the other person to become frustrated or anxious which, in turn, could result in the other person walking out. If anger is used against you, you may be able to take advantage of it. Listen carefully to the outburst's substance. You might try showing that you are personally hurt by the outburst. Making the other person feel guilty may help you control their anger by simply embarrassing them. In any event, your response should normally be temperate. Think twice before you respond in kind. Escalation might result in the breakdown of the negotiation and seriously interfere with the ability to start discussions later.

2. Aggression

Aggressive behavior, like anger, is designed to intimidate. As with anger, a more temperate response is usually appropriate. You might try to control the behavior by conducting the negotiation in a way that minimizes its impact. Similarly, it is harder to be aggressive with other people present, so negotiating in a team might be helpful. Likewise, it is harder to be aggressive and, of course, easier for you to terminate the meeting, if the negotiation takes place on the telephone. Negotiating at the aggressive lawyer's office might be appropriate because it makes it easier for you to terminate the session by walking out if the aggression becomes intolerable.

3. Boulwareism

Boulwareism is a tactic named after a former vice president of General Electric. The tactic involves making one offer, demand, or proposal and then never making a concession. It is really a take it or leave it tactic. The theory is that you will have gained sufficient information before making the proposal that you can communicate your best offer up front.

Looking at the tactic in light of our systematic approach, it may take considerable education on your part to convince the person you are serious. You will need to persuade the other person not only that the first offer is fair, just, and equitable, but that there is indeed no more. Most people think that a controlling principle of negotiations is that first offers are always negotiable, and you may have difficulty persuading someone that this convention does not apply.

A very real problem with this tactic is in formulating an appropriate take it or leave it offer. Negotiation is a fluid process. As you gather information, not just in formal information bargaining, but through making offers and counter-offers, as well as persuasive statements, you continually gather more information that eventually gives you the confidence to know what is truly the best proposal for you.

If you use Boulwareism you must also be prepared to stick to it. If you ever make a concession, your credibility is seriously impaired.

4. Balance or Slightly Outnumber the Other Side

Often it is suggested that you will gain an advantage in the negotiation by balancing your side's negotiators or outnumbering the other side. This may be useful. Again, going back to the systematic approach, we can see that there may be advantages. As we pointed out in Chapter 3, you cannot ignore the social-psychological dynamic of the negotiation process. Having an equal number of negotiators may very well make you less intimidated and therefore more effective. Likewise, outnumbering the other side may well increase their anxiety.

Such tactics, however, carry a downside. If your goal is to be a cooperative problem solver, such a tactic could destroy the relationship you are trying to achieve. Multiple negotiators, however, may be useful for other purposes. As seen from the above discussion, many competing demands are placed on a negotiator—listening, asking questions, responding to questions, and formulating proposals. Sharing these responsibilities can be a great help. Assigning a secondary negotiator the task of simply listening is useful. Periodic caucuses in which the negotiators compare notes on what has been said may give the principal negotiator a better perspective on the changing dynamic of the negotiation itself.

On the other hand, having a single negotiator has a number of advantages. A single person prevents the other side from taking advantage of potential divisions such as differences of opinion. A single negotiator places complete responsibility on one person and minimizes missteps by one negotiator interfering with the actions of a partner. A single negotiator may also find it easier to take advantage of unexpected opportunities.

A variation on the multiple negotiator is often called Mutt and Jeff or Good Cop/Bad Cop. In this situation, one negotiator appears reasonable and sympathetic while the other is demanding and aggressive. The demanding, aggressive person quickly rejects proposals and the other attempts to reach an agreement. The sympathetic negotiator then suggests concessions that might bridge the gap between his own partner and the person with whom they are negotiating. The tactic, which appears so blatantly manipulative on paper, can be used with incredible success by many negotiators and is quite popular.

5. False Demands

Demanding something the person doesn't really want is another common tactic. By communicating the false demand along with the real demands, the negotiator establishes a bargaining chip to be later traded away. Viewed in our systematic approach, a risk of this tactic is that if you are not as persuasive with this demand as all your other demands, it will be clear that it is false. In turn, you must not give it up without good reason. Finally, be prepared to face the fact that if you ask for it, you might get it.

6. First Offer

It is often said that you should never make the first offer in negotiation. As with most rules, there is an element of truth to this rule, but it is also terribly misleading. Quite often, you have no choice but to make the first offer. If, for example, you are selling something, you will normally be expected to set the asking price. While it may not be impossible to get the buyer to make the first offer, it is unusual.

Asking why a rule such as this developed is helpful in deciding its utility. In other words, what is the risk of making the first offer? Typically the risk is that you will underestimate your position and ask for too little. The great fear in buying a house, for example, is that the seller will take your first offer and you will feel you offered too much.

Once again, thinking in terms of our systematic approach, the risk in making the first offer is that you might make it before you have sufficient information to assess the relative positions of the negotiators. The risk is not in making the first offer, but in making the first offer with insufficient information. In other words, the advantage of getting the other side to make the first offer is that they may prematurely move from the information bargaining stage into proposal stage.

As you gain information, the risk of making the first offer decreases. If you are in a situation where it appears inevitable that you will have to make the first offer, it merely emphasizes the importance of approaching the negotiation systematically; that is, to be sure to engage in adequate information bargaining before the proposal is made.

A common example of the difficulty is where a person quickly brushes off ice breaking and says, "That's great, but let's get to the point." Here is, in our framework, an attempt to get the lawyer to skip information bargaining. If the lawyer makes an offer now, there is a high risk that the lawyer will offer more than is required. The lawyer must exercise agenda control to move the process back and complete the information bargaining. For example, the lawyer might say:

> *Well, I'm certainly here to see if we can do business. The fact is, though, I'll need lots of information before I can make a judgment about whether that's even possible. Why don't we do this. You've sent me some helpful information, but let me ask you some questions to clarify some things and find some new pieces. Then I'll be in a better position to see what we can do. For example, tell me something about . . . .*

7. Never Negotiate Against Yourself

Negotiating against yourself is where you have made an offer that has been rejected and then, before the other side makes a counter offer, you make a concession. Again, the rule that you should never do this has a legitimate basis under our systematic approach. As discussed concerning concessions, you should never concede without having been persuaded that something about your initial justification may have been in error. Making a concession for no reason other than the fact that the other side rejected your previous proposal seriously affects the credibility of the original offer and all subsequent offers.

8. Telephone Negotiations

The reality is that much negotiation takes place on the telephone. Economic necessity mandates that person-to-person meetings cannot always be held. Telephone conversations are inherently less personal and, therefore, the other negotiator will be more likely to not treat you as another human being, and perhaps more likely to be adversarial, competitive, and even deceptive. Nonverbal communication becomes even more important, and you must pay careful attention to the pitch, pace, tone, and volume of the other person's voice.

If you initiate a telephone negotiation you must be as prepared as if you were negotiating face-to-face. Also, just as you should not meet someone face-to-face without preparation, if you receive an unexpected telephone call and the other side wishes to negotiate, you should feel little obligation to engage in meaningful discussion if you are unprepared.

9. Time Pressure

Setting an artificial time frame can be a useful tactic. Remember from Chapter 3 that time pressures tend to make people's aspirations, demands, and bluffing decrease. Where someone is very interested in making a deal, the deadline's pressure might result in concessions that otherwise would not occur.

On the other hand, where possible, you should try not to communicate if you have time pressures that the other person does not share. Also, where an artificial time pressure has been imposed—accept by today or we withdraw the offer—ask yourself how credible the limitation is. Finally, do not reveal to the other side any time deadlines you may be under to wrap up a deal because they may seek to use the deadline to their advantage.

The above discussion should place the exchange phase of the negotiation, and what occurs therein, in context. The next chapter will address the final phase of the negotiation.

Chapter 8

CRISIS AND OUTCOME

A. Crisis

Crisis is the point in the negotiation at which the parties either agree or deadlock. Aside from making concessions which might destroy the value of an agreement for your side, there is no sure way to avoid deadlock. In the real world, not all deals are meant to happen. In adversarial negotiating terms, the parties' bargaining ranges may simply not overlap. In problem-solving negotiation, the parties may simply be unable to come up with a solution acceptable to all.

Where deadlock appears imminent do not simply give up. As with any problem in negotiation, ask yourself what is causing the problem? Here again, the systematic approach helps.

1. Check Whether There Has Been a Failure of Process

Many negotiations deadlock because a failure has occurred in one stage or another in the negotiation process. Ask whether a problem exists with one of the stages. Have tensions resulted in a relationship among the negotiators that prevents agreement? Has animosity grown to the point that the reason there will be no agreement is that people do not like each other? The parties have failed to develop the appropriate relationship and time might be well spent trying to foster that relationship. A failure may have occurred in the information bargaining stage. If the parties, for example, cannot agree on the actual market value of an item, there may be no chance of reaching agreement. Is there a neutral way of determining market rate? Perhaps you have not been persuasive. Have you or your opponent made irrational concessions, attempted to split the difference perhaps, and therefore been unable to persuade each other that you are indeed at your bottom line? Stopping to assess the negotiation in terms of the stages may help you respond to the impending deadlock, or prevent it entirely.

117

2. Consider Changing Strategy

If you are an adversarial negotiator, as deadlock approaches, you should probably consider a fundamental change in strategy. Remember from Chapter 1 that what makes problem-solving particularly effective is trust or little risk. Has trust developed, or is there no risk, so that you can move to problem-solving? Or, if deadlock is near and you really need to reach an agreement, ask yourself if you will lose anything by abandoning your position, expressing your needs, interests, and desires, and seeking a problem-solving solution. Of course, you will not always overcome the deadlock, but you have little to lose at this point by focusing the discussion on underlying needs.

3. Third Party Intervention: Alternate Dispute Resolution

In certain circumstances, you may avoid deadlock by involving third parties such as mediators. Where the negotiation involves a dispute between the parties, and negotiation does not appear to be able to settle the dispute, you might consider some form of alternate dispute resolution. Use of alternate dispute resolution may be particularly appropriate where the dispute can escalate into an expensive, time consuming, emotionally draining lawsuit.

A complete discussion of the various forms of alternate dispute resolution is beyond the scope of this book,[20] however, it may be useful to have a basic understanding of what various options are available. Typically, privately arranged alternate dispute resolution includes negotiation as well as:

- arbitration, both binding and non-binding;
- mediation;
- summary jury trials/mini-trials;
- a combination of some or all of the above.

These types of third party intervention may be effective because each helps to:

1. reduce irrationality;

2. reduce impact of social-psychological influences;

3. explore alternative solutions;

4. provide opportunities for graceful retreat; and

---

20. For a complete discussion, see J. Cooley, *A Practical Guide to Mediation and Arbitration Advocacy* (NITA, 1996).

5. facilitate communication.

a. Arbitration

Arbitration is typically viewed as an alternative to litigation. In essence, arbitration is a private form of litigation in which the parties choose the person who, after hearing some form of presentation from each side of the dispute, renders a decision much as a judge would. The theory is that a neutral third party in a private setting has several advantages, including:

- the parties can select an arbitrator that has particular experience with the type of issues raised in the dispute;
- the dispute can be resolved privately, thus avoiding much of the adverse publicity associated with a public lawsuit;
- the arbitration tends to be more informal, and it is even possible for the parties to represent themselves rather than hire an attorney;
- arbitration can be completed more quickly than a lawsuit;
- arbitration may save money.

Arbitration is based on an agreement of the parties. As such, the parties can tailor the arbitration to a large extent based on the particular needs of the dispute. A primary point of agreement will have to be whether the arbitration will be binding or non-binding. The parties can agree that the arbitrator's decision is binding and hence enforceable against the losing party. On the other hand, they can agree that the result is non-binding. If the decision is non-binding, the result is in effect advisory and, hence, may suggest to the losing party that they should not pursue the matter through litigation because they will probably lose.

b. Mediation

Mediation is the process by which a neutral third party assists the parties to the dispute in resolving the matter. A mediator has no authority to impose a solution and often does not even propose solutions, but rather assists the parties to come to their own agreement. Since the parties normally must agree to mediation, as with arbitration you can tailor the precise role of the mediator to a specific problem.

c. Summary Jury Trials/Mini Trials

As a variation on a form of arbitration, trials by private judges are becoming more popular. The precise name given to these private trials varies depending on the particular ground rules established, but in general, each method relies upon a private judge to conduct a form of trial. The trial is often an abbreviated version of what would happen in court. The abbreviations might consist of presenting testimony in summary form, or in limiting the time available to each side to present evidence. A particularly creative variation is to conduct such a mini-trial and, rather than having the judge make a decision, the disputants return to the negotiation table to see if they can settle the dispute with their new awareness of how the trial might go.

B. The Outcome

Every negotiation is unique when it comes to the specifics of what makes a good outcome. There are, however, a number of general considerations to keep in mind. The outcome should, in no particular order:

- reflect the parties' goals and authority;
- create a minimum of new problems;
- be efficient;
- be achievable;
- be enforceable;
- be implementable;
- be fair, just, and equitable;
- have the desired level of specificity/ambiguity;
- be comprehensive;
- anticipate contingencies.

C. Wrap-up

The negotiation as a whole, and individual sessions of a negotiation must be ended just as they must begin. Parties often forget that ending entails a number of concerns. First, just as you want to start the negotiation setting the proper tone, you want to end it with the appropriate tone. People tend to remember most what they hear first and last, so the ending should involve rapport building (or perhaps rebuilding).

On a substantive level the wrap-up should include a summary of the work completed to that point, and if the negotiation is complete, you should completely restate the agreement reached. If additional negotiation is required, you should summarize progress to date so that there will be less chance of misinterpretation at the next session.

At the end of each session, each party should have a clear understanding of what their next step will be and when the next meeting (or how it will be determined) will take place. If the other person has indicated during the negotiation that she will provide you with certain financial information, for example, you must reiterate that promise and establish a specific time frame. If you have promised to do something, restate that commitment and time frame.

D. Memorialization

In today's world, almost any negotiation, especially one involving lawyers, will end with some form of writing that is a contract or summary of the negotiation. Given the free flowing nature of negotiation and the limitations of the human mind, often when someone sits down to summarize the agreement certain issues will remain unresolved, or at least their resolution is ambiguous. Given this circumstance, it makes sense that you should do the summary yourself, if possible. This allows you the first opportunity to resolve these issues or ambiguities. Presenting your resolution to the other side is, in a sense, establishing the agenda for resolution of these hopefully minor issues.

Chapter 9

ETHICAL CONSIDERATIONS

Usually, negotiators prefer not to disclose everything at a negotiation's outset, and want to influence the direction the negotiation goes to some extent. Even cooperative problem solvers do not initially disclose everything and are interested in steering the negotiation, or at least the process the negotiation follows, in a particular direction. Competitive adversarial negotiators might be more blunt. They seek to mislead the other side, at least as to their real bottom line, and they seek to manipulate the other side to achieve their goals. Given this setting, that negotiation raises a number of ethical issues should not be a surprise. Chief among the ethical issues in negotiation is how truthful you must be. In this chapter we will discuss this issue and raise additional ethical considerations of which you should be aware.

A. Truthfulness

The most troubling ethical issue in negotiation is lying. A fundamental assumption of negotiation is that the participants resist revealing at least some information to the other side. To be sure, during information bargaining, adversarials emphasize seeking and hiding information whereas problem solvers emphasize seeking and revealing information. In Chapter 6, we discussed the tactics associated with "blocking" the disclosure of information. At what point does this attempt to avoid disclosure become unethical? Unfortunately, no clear answer exists.

123

Problem 9.1

The lawyers for Parker & Gould have been authorized to settle the lawsuit with Margaret Polisi for no more than $500,000. During face-to-face negotiations, may the lawyers for Parker & Gould, ethically state: "My client has authorized to settle for nothing more than $250,000. That's our bottom line. Accept it or we will see you in court."?

Problem 9.1 raises the basic question of whether negotiation statements concerning what your client will find acceptable are subject to a truthfulness standard. The American Bar Association Model Rules of Professional Conduct and its precursor the Model Code of Professional Responsibility provide only general statements concerning the obligation to be truthful. Model Rule 4.1 provides:

In the course of representing a client a lawyer shall not:

(a) Knowingly make a false statement of fact or law to a third person; or

(b) Knowingly fail to disclose a fact to a third person when:

(1) In the circumstances failure to make disclosure is equivalent to making a material misrepresentation;

(2) Disclosure is necessary to prevent assisting a criminal or fraudulent act, as required by Rule 1.2(d); or

(3) Disclosure is necessary to comply with the law.

Model Rule 4.1(b) provides little more guidance than the admonition that lawyers shall not fail to disclose when such failure is in violation of legal requirements to disclose. Subparagraph (a), however, with its broad prohibition against making a false statement has significantly more potential for suggesting ethical restrictions. What the drafters actually contemplated by the phrase "knowingly make a false statement" is, however, not at all clear. A comment to Rule 4.1 in fact states, "Under generally accepted conventions in negotiation, certain types of statements ordinarily are not taken as statements of material fact. Estimates of price or value placed on the subject of a transaction and a party's intentions as to an acceptable settlement of a claim are in this category . . . ."

Under the commentary to the Model Rules, it appears clear that counsel's statements in Problem 9.1 are ethically permissible. However, relying on conventions—as the community does—to determine what is permissible is problematic at best. A number of problems are readily apparent. What community of lawyers should we look at to determine the conventions? Do the conventions in one geographical area apply across the country, much less the state or the city? Even within a geographical area do lawyers in different types of practices have different conventions? Are the conventions different for criminal defense attorneys, for example, than for securities lawyers?

In light of the ambiguity of the standard, a couple of points must be made. First, you should not assume that your interpretation of existing conventions is the same as opposing counsel's. A little skepticism is not a bad thing. Certain conduct crosses the line and constitutes unethical or even illegal behavior. However, you should recognize that negotiation is among the most private activities a lawyer does and you cannot count on the bar ethics committee to be looking over your opponent's shoulder.

Second, some guidance is nonetheless available. The Model Rule's commentary that "[e]stimates of price or value placed on the subject of a transaction and a party's intentions as to an acceptable settlement of a claim are in this category . . . ." suggests that a useful distinction can be made between statements concerning historical facts on the one hand and interpretations, inferences, or intentions. A statement that a client has received twenty stitches as a result of the accident when he only received ten concerns a historic, objectively verifiable fact, and is a lie. A statement that the client will not accept less than $200,000 in satisfaction of his claim, when after counseling, the client has indicated he would accept as little as $50,000, is puffing and would generally be considered permissible.

B. Other Ethical Considerations

A number of other professional responsibility issues, none unique to negotiation should be kept in mind.

Model Rules of Professional Conduct Rule 1.1 provides that "[a] lawyer shall provide competent representation to a client. Competent representation requires the legal knowledge, skill, thoroughness and preparation reasonably necessary for the representation." The obligation to provide competent representation obviously is not unique to negotiation. You should remember, however, that competence is more than facility with doctrinal analysis. Competence in the context of a negotiation requires negotiation skill, just as competence in the context of a trial lawyer requires courtroom skill.

Problem 9.2

Assume in Problem 9.1 plaintiff's counsel responds by saying, "That offer is insulting. I'm not even going to dignify it by taking it back to my client." **Is there an ethical problem?**

To the extent that the lawyer in Problem 9.2 does not take the settlement offer back to Polisi, there appears to be an ethical problem. Model Rules of Professional Conduct Rule 1.2(a) provides that "[a] lawyer shall abide by a client's decision whether to accept an offer of settlement of a matter. In a criminal case, the lawyer shall abide by the client's decision, after consultation with the lawyer, as to a plea to be entered, whether to waive jury trial and whether the client will testify." The Model Rules clearly make the decision on whether to accept a legitimate settlement offer the client's—not the lawyer's. Indeed, the Model Rules make it clear that the lawyer has an affirmative obligation to ensure that the client has sufficient information upon which to base this decision: "a lawyer negotiating on behalf of a client should provide the client with facts relevant to the matter, inform the client of communications from another party and take other reasonable steps that permit the client to make a decision regarding a serious offer from another party." Model Rules of Professional Conduct Rule 1.4.

Problem 9.3

Assume that in Problem 9.2 defense counsel is convinced that plaintiff's counsel has not communicated the $250,000 offer to Polisi. May defense counsel contact her directly with the offer?

As just discussed, Model Rules 1.2 and 1.4 require a client's decision concerning a serious settlement offer. Problem 9.3, however, raises the question of what can be done by opposing counsel if she believes the offer has not been communicated to the other party. On occasion a lawyer will feel frustrated, thinking that a legitimate offer they have put on the table has not been taken back to the client. The solution is, however, not to bypass opposing counsel and communicate directly to the opposing party. Model Rules of Professional Conduct Rule 4.2 states: "In representing a client, a lawyer shall not communicate about the subject of the representation with a party the lawyer knows to be represented by another lawyer in the matter, unless the lawyer has the consent of the other lawyer or is authorized by law to do so."

The options available to you to get the offer to an opposing party are therefore limited. Asking your client to contact the other client is not an option in a litigation setting, since you cannot circumvent an ethical proscription through the actions of a third person. If suit has been filed and the jurisdiction has a provision similar to Federal Rule of Civil Procedure 68's offer of judgment, invoking the rule may provide some help in this situation. Rule 68 provides in part, "[a]t any time more than 10 days before the trial begins, a party defending against a claim may serve upon the adverse party an offer to allow judgment . . . against the defending party . . . for the money . . . specified in the offer." If the offer is not accepted, and the offeree ultimately recovers less than the offer, the offeree must pay all costs subsequent to the offer. The effect of the provision for our purposes is that it increases the likelihood opposing counsel will at least communicate an offer made subject to Rule 68.

General provisions concerning confidentiality and conflict of interest, of course, affect the lawyer in negotiation. In particular, Model Rules of Professional Conduct Rule 1.8(g) provides that "[a] lawyer who represents two or more clients shall not participate in making an aggregate settlement of the claims of or against the clients . . . unless each client consents after consultation, including disclosure of the existence and nature of all the claims . . . involved and the participation of each person in the settlement." This Rule makes clear what should probably already be clear from general provisions governing conflicts of interest and the client's right to accept or reject settlement offers.

A final consideration concerns Model Rules of Professional Conduct Rule 4.4, which prohibits conduct intended to humiliate and harass. Competitive negotiators, in particular, must be aware of the line between aggressive advocacy and harassment. Crossing that line may not only affect your effectiveness, but be unethical.

C. Conclusion

As much if not more than anything else a lawyer does, negotiation is usually a very private activity. The client is counseled in private and the lawyers sit down face-to-face in private. The result may be public, but the process is quite closed. As such, inappropriate behavior will not likely be subject to outside review. Just imagine, for example, the difficulty of filing a complaint with a state bar ethics group and then proving that opposing counsel has lied to you during the negotiation. Negotiation, like so much else a lawyer does, therefore, relies heavily on the individual ethics of the participants involved. You should keep in mind that your ethical conduct with a client or an opponent in a negotiation will pay dividends to both your professional reputation and your future dealings with these people.

APPENDIX

PREPARATION AND PLANNING WORKSHEET

Your Goals

— What do you wish to accomplish?

— What are you willing to accept?

Their Goals

— What do you believe the other party seeks to accomplish?

— What do you believe the other party would be willing to accept?

Adversarial or problem-solving or a combination?

— What advantages do each strategy have in this particular negotiation?

— If you are going to approach the negotiation from an adversarial perspective, what is your bottom line at this point?

— What will you use as a starting position?

— What facts do you have that might indicate

  • the likely starting position of the other side?

  • the likely bottom line of the other side?

— Can you plot the potential bargaining ranges on each side?

— **What information do you have available that would suggest the other side's probable strategy (adversarial, problem-solving or some mix)?**

> — What facts do you have that might indicate
>
> - the underlying needs, interests and desires of the other side?
> - the probable proposals the other side might make?

— **Are you aware of any social or psychological facts that might impact this negotiation?**

— **If you are willing to shift strategy during the negotiation, what factors will motivate you to switch? How will you make the switch?**

> For example, if you wish to move from adversarial to problem-solving, what actions can you plan to take to increase trust or decrease the risk associated with problem-solving?

— **What information can you seek from sources other than a face- to-face meeting with the other person?**

— **Is this negotiation best accomplished face-to-face, by telephone, by letter, or some combination? Why?**

— **If the negotiation is face-to-face, where will it take place? Why?**

— **If you control the setting of the negotiation, how will you arrange the location?**

PREPARATION AND PLANNING WORKSHEET

— How long will the negotiation take? Why?

— In this particular phase of the negotiation do you seek to accomplish all of your goals, or will this have a more limited purpose? For example, is this meeting only to obtain information or merely to begin developing a rapport?

— Are there any conventions or controlling principles you need to consider in this negotiation?

— How will you establish the agenda?

> — How will you establish what to negotiate?

> — How will you establish the manner in which you negotiate?

— What type of ice breaking will you use, if any? Why?

— What information do you need to get from the other person? Why?

> — How will you get this information?

> — What questions will you ask to get information from the other person?

> — In what order will you ask the questions?

> — What information is the other side likely to seek from you?

> — What information is the other side likely to try and avoid giving you?

> — What will you do if the other person asks you for information you do not want to reveal?

— What will you do if the person refuses to give you a piece of information either by blocking or outright refusal?

— What will you do if the person tells you what you know to be a lie?

— What information do you need to give the other side and how will you give it?

— What type of persuasive statements will you make?

— Can you identify objective criteria that supports the likely positions you will take or proposed solutions you will make?

— What are the possible criteria to be used by the other side?

— How will you respond to them?

— What are the details of your persuasive elements?

— Can you make your persuasive statements multidimensional? balanced? emphatic?

— Are there any points that must be subtle?

— Do you anticipate any threats?

— How will you respond to threats?

— What type of concessions are you willing to consider?

— What will you need to convince you a concession is appropriate?

PREPARATION AND PLANNING WORKSHEET

— How will you respond if any of the following tactics is used against you?

Anger

Aggression

Boulwareism

Uneven number of negotiators

False demands

Attempts to get you to make the first offer

Attempts to get you to negotiate against yourself

Time pressure

— Will you use any of these tactics? Why?

— If it appears you are going to deadlock, what might you do?

— When will you likely end this negotiation?

— How will you likely end this negotiation?

POST NEGOTIATION WORKSHEET

Did you accomplish your goals? Why? Why not?

Were you able to set the tone that you desired for the negotiation? Why or why not?

Did you control the agenda? Why or why not?

Did you find as much information as you wanted? Why or why not?

Did you reveal too much information? Why or why not?

Did you fail to reveal information you should have? Why or why not?

If you did not agree, was it appropriate given the context of this particular negotiation? Why or why not?

If you have deadlocked, what might you be able to do to break that deadlock? Why or why not?

If you agreed, is the result fair, just and equitable from everyone's perspective? Why or why not?

For each stage of the negotiation process that you conducted, what did you learn from this negotiation:

Preparation and Planning

Ice Breaking

Agenda Control

Information Bargaining

Offers/Demands/Proposals

Persuasion

Concessions/reformulations

Crisis

Closing

Memorialization

What is the one thing you will do differently in the next negotiation?
Why?

SELECTED BIBLIOGRAPHY

The following list of articles and books is not meant to be an exhaustive bibliography. Also, the list is not meant to imply I agree with what the material has to say about negotiation. In fact, I do not agree with everything that is said in these books and articles, but they provide additional detail, and sometimes a different perspective which can further your understanding of the negotiation process.

Articles

Berman, *Facilitated Negotiation: An Effective ADR Technique*, 50 Disp. Resol. J. 18 (1995).

Berman, *Facilitating Construction Negotiations*, 50 Disp. Resol. J. 23 (1995).

Brazil, *Protecting the Confidentiality of Settlement Negotiations*, 39 Hastings L.J. 955 (1988).

Cash and Janda, "The Eye of the Beholder," *Psychology Today* 46 (December 1984).

Condlin, *Bargaining in the Dark: The Normative Incoherence of Lawyer Dispute Bargaining Role,* 51 Md. L. Rev. 1 (1992).

Condlin, *"Cases on Both Sides": Patterns of Argument in Legal Dispute Negotiation*, 44 Md. L. Rev, 65 (1985).

Cooley, *The Geometries of Situation and Emotions and the Calculus of Change in Negotiation and Mediation*, 29 Val. U. L. Rev. 1 (1994).

Daugherty and Reinganum, *Settlement Negotiations with Two-sided Asymmetric Information: Model Duality, Information Distribution, and Efficiency*, 14 Int'l Rev. L. & Econ. 283 (1994).

Farmer and Pecorino, *Pretrial Negotiations with Asymmetric Information on Risk Preferences*, 14 Int'l, Rev. L. & Econ. 273 (1994).

Gifford, *The Synthesis of Legal Counseling and Negotiation Models: Preserving Client-centered Advocacy in the Negotiation Context*, 34 UCLA L. Rev. 811 (1987).

Gross and Syverud, *Getting to No: A Study of Settlement Negotiations and the Selection of Cases for Trial*, 90 Mich. L. Rev. 319 (1991).

Guernsey, *Truthfulness in Negotiation*, 17 U. Rich. L. Rev. 99 (1982).

Hogan, *Judicial Settlement Conferences: Empowering the Parties to Decide Through Negotiation*, 27 Willamette L. Rev. 429 (1991).

Hyman, *Trial Advocacy and Methods of Negotiation: Can Good Trial Advocates Be Wise Negotiators?* 34 U.C.L.A.L. Rev. 863 (1987).

Kuklin, *The Asymmetrical Conditions of Legal Responsibility in the Marketplace*, 44 U. Miami L. Rev. 893 (1990).

Lerman, *Lying to Clients*, 138 U. Pa. L. Rev. 659 (1990).

Lowenthal, *A General Theory of Negotiation Process, Strategy and Behavior*, 31 U. Kan. Law Rev. 69 (1982).

McMunigal, *Disclosure and Accuracy in the Guilty Plea Process*, 40 Hastings L.J. 957 (1989).

Menkel-Meadow, *Toward Another View of Legal Negotiation: The Structure of problem-solving*, 31 U.C.L.A. Law Review 754 (1984).

Norton, *Bargaining and the Ethic of Process*, 64 N.Y.U.L. Rev. 493 (1989).

Perschbacher, *Regulating Lawyers' Negotiations*, 27 Ariz. L. Rev. 75 (1985).

Peters, *Forever Jung: Psychological Type Theory, the Myers-Briggs Type Indicator and Learning Negotiation*, 42 Drake L. Rev. 1 (1993).

Peters, *The Use of Lies in Negotiation*, 48 Ohio St. L.J. 1 (1987).

Rubin, *A Causerie on Lawyers' Ethics in Negotiation*, 35 La. L. Rev. 577 (1975).

Wetlaufer, *The Ethics of Lying in Negotiations*, 75 Iowa L. Rev. 1219 (1990).

Wilkins, *Plea Negotiations, Acceptance of Responsibility, Role of the Offender, and Departures: Policy Decisions in the Promulgation of Federal Sentencing Guidelines*, 23 Wake Forest L. Rev. 181 (1988).

Selected Books

Bacharach, S. & Lawler, E., *Bargaining: Power Tactics and Outcomes* (1981).

Bastrass, R. & Harbaugh, J., *Interviewing, Counseling, and Negotiating* (1990).

Berne, E., *Games People Play* (1964).

Bok, S., *Lying: Moral Choice in Public and Private Life* (1978).

Benjamin, A., *The Helping Interview* (1974).

Brooks, E., & Odiorne, G., *Managing by Negotiations* (1984).

Cohen, H., *You Can Negotiate Anything* (1980).

Craver, C., *Effective Legal Negotiation and Settlement*, (2d ed. 1993).

Cross, J., *Economics of Bargaining* (1969).

Druckman, D., *Negotiations: Social Psychological Perspectives* (1977).

Druckman, D., Rozelle, G., & Baxter, J., *Nonverbal Communication: Survey, Theory and Research* (1982).

Fast, J., *Body Language* (Pocket Books 1970).

Fisher, R., Ury, W., *Getting to Yes: Negotiating Agreement Without Giving In* (1981).

Gifford, D., *Legal Negotiation: Theory and Applications* (1989)

Goldberg, S., Green, E., & Sander, F., *Dispute Resolution* (1985).

Hall, E., *The Silent Language* (1959).

Hall, J., *Nonverbal Sex Differences* (1984).

Haydock, R., *Negotiation Practice* (1984).

Henley, N., *Body, Politics, Sex, and Nonverbal Communication* (1977).

Jandt, F., *Win-Win Negotiating; Turning Conflict into Agreement* (1985).

Harper, R., Wiens, A., & Matarazzo, J., *Nonverbal Communication: The State of the Art* (1978).

Karrass, C., *Give and Take* (1974).

Karrass, C., *The Negotiating Game* (1970).

Karrass, G., *Negotiate to Close* (1985).

Korda, M., *Power! How to Get It, How to Use It* (1975).

Kuhn, R., *Dealmaker: All the Negotiating Skills and Secrets You Need* (1988).

Lax, D., *The Manager as Negotiator: Bargaining for Cooperation and Competitive Gain* (1986).

Lesti, P., Danninger, B., & Johnson, R., *Structured Settlements* (1986).

Mehrabian, A., *Nonverbal Communication* (1972).

_____. *Silent Messages: Implicit Communication of Emotions and Attitudes* (1981).

Morrison, W., *The Prenegotiation Planning Book* (1985).

Nierenberg, G., *The Art of Negotiating* (1987). 6 cassettes and workbook.

_____. *The Complete Negotiator* (1986).

_____. *Fundamentals of Negotiating* (1973).

Nierenberg, G. & Calero, H., *How to Read a Person Like a Book* (1971).

Personal Injury Valuation Handbooks (Jury Verdict Research, Inc.).

Richardson, L., *Winning Negotiation Strategies for Bankers* (1987).

Ringer, R., *Winning Through Intimidation* (1974).

Rubin, J. & Brown, B., *The Social Psychology of Bargaining and Negotiation* (1975).

Siegel, S., & Fouraker, L., *Bargaining and Group Decision Making* (1976).

Sperber, P., *Attorney's Practice Guide to Negotiations* (1985).

Strauss, A., *Negotiations: Varieties, Contexts, Processes, and Social Order* (1978).

Teply, *Legal Negotiation in a Nutshell* (1992).

Von Neumann, J., & Morgenstern, O., *Theory of Games and Economic Behavior* (1944).

Williams, G., *Legal Negotiation and Settlement* (1983).

_____, *Effective Negotiation and Settlement* (1981).

INDEX